Scapegoating in Families

Intergenerational Patterns of
Physical and Emotional Abuse

Scapegoating in Families

*Intergenerational Patterns of
Physical and Emotional Abuse*

Vimala Pillari, D.S.W.

BRUNNER/MAZEL, *Publishers* · NEW YORK

Library of Congress Cataloging-in-Publication Data
Pillari, Vimala.
    Scapegoating in families : intergenerational patterns of physical
and emotional abuse / Vimala Pillari.
        p.   cm.
    Includes bibliographical references and index.
    ISBN 0-87630-639-3
    1. Abused children—Mental health.   2. Psychologically abused
children—Mental health.   3. Scapegoat—Psychological aspects.
4. Parent and child.   5. Problem families.   I. Title.
RJ507.A29P55   1991
618.92'85822—dc20   91-3452
                                                              CIP

Published by
BRUNNER/MAZEL, INC.
19 Union Square West
New York, New York 10003

Manufactured in the United States of America

Designed by M. Franklin-Plympton

10 9 8 7 6 5 4 3 2 1

Dedicated to
Dr. Moses Newsome Jr.

Goodness and decency have no boundaries.

Contents

Foreword

The literature on the physical and emotional abuse of children continues to grow rapidly. It alerts us to frightening human experiences and conditions that require exploration, while inflaming passions and triggering accusations and counteraccusations. The needed exploration is made more difficult by the fact that it has to be carried out from divergent vantage points and with the help of concepts that derive from differing contexts and origins. These concepts open up certain perspectives and inquiries while they shut off others that may be equally relevant.

Dr. Vimala Pillari, the author of this volume, had to grapple with this quandary also. She chose the concepts of *scapegoat* and *scapegoating* as her vantage points for the exploration of the phenomena under discussion—a choice that strikes me as felicitous. It facilitates a presentation and an analysis that are penetrating as well as refreshing.

The scapegoat is also called a burden-bearer. As such, he or she can be compared to what I described as a delegate. Both concepts refer to persons who impress us as having been or are still being abused and exploited. But instead of openly rebelling against such abuse and exploitation, they are likely to turn into obedient victims. And often, so it seems, they take care of their exploiters, defend and protect them, and try to absolve them of guilt. How is this possible?

In offering her answer to this and other pertinent questions, Dr. Pillari focuses on the intrapsychic as well as interpersonal processes that come into play by drawing on insights derived from psychoanalysis and systems theory. At the same time, she reveals herself as a skillful and dedicated therapist. Last but not least, she provides us with a concise introduction into the fundamentals of an intergenerational view of families and the treatment problems revealed by such an approach. As in her earlier book, *Pathways to Family Myths*, Dr. Pillari has succeeded in writing a text that is highly readable, illuminating, and therapeutically inspiring.

HELM STIERLIN, M.D., PH.D.
Medical Director
Department of Family Therapy
University of Heidelberg Medical School
West Germany

Acknowledgments

My deep gratitude to my clients, the scapegoated and the scapegoaters, from whom I learned about the intricacies of being part of a different family system in all its pain, sadness, and complications. It has been a growing experience for me.

My heartfelt thanks to Dr. Isaac Alcabes, State University at Buffalo, New York, for his complete and caring support, intellectual stimulation, and constructive criticisms; and to Rebecca O. Barclay, Rensselaer Polytechnic Institute, New York, for her support and editing.

Special thanks to Natalie Gilman from Brunner/Mazel, for her whole-hearted support, sprinkled with humor and masterful guidance.

Thanks to you, too, Steve and Kapil.

Introduction

Scapegoated children aroused my curiosity. A family would present for therapy with the finger pointed at one child, and the child would, as if by magic, play the role so well. Yet the family and child suffered. Studying these families and their adult or young children in therapy moved me to analyze intently a variety of family experiences in which scapegoating occurred. I can now empathize with the scapegoat and understand the scapegoat's dysfunctional relationships.

FAMILY LIFE AND DIFFERENCES

In families of severely scapegoated children, difficulties arise from many causes. Therefore, whenever possible, I have gone to great lengths to illuminate the complexity of human behavior and family dynamics.

How different are families of severely scapegoated children from functional families? In reality, I believe the main difference is that they constantly go to extremes and behave in ways that are upsetting to others and to themselves. But otherwise they are similar to everyone else in most of their activities. A great deal of their behavior is seen within the "average, normal range," and they follow routines of life just like other people.

What is the reality of these families? Is their family culture totally different? When we meet any member from a scapegoating family, does the question "How different is he or she from me?" arise? Although members of scapegoating families have problems in their lives, their dreams and hopes are not very different from other families/people. If we all share similar dreams and hopes, then we have something in common. In my therapeutic work, thinking of commonalities was very helpful, for it seemed to increase my sensitivity and empathy for the scapegoated individuals. It also led me to understand that although two cultures may seem very different from the outside, with their different lifestyles and backgrounds, people basically have similar dreams, illusions, and hopes about life.

BLAMING THE VICTIM

This book focuses on severely scapegoated individuals. Those of us who work with severely scapegoated persons know that it is easy to blame the parent or the child. Blame is a kind of incrimination because it implies that the parent deliberately hates the child. Some therapists blame the child for the parents' disturbances, the reasoning being that the child was very difficult in her or his behavior and drove the parents out of control. In this book you will notice that parents and their children are the victims of their upbringing. Whenever there was a revelation of their own family history, it showed that the parents as children were victimized and ill-treated by their own parents. In turn, these adult children of such parents abused their own children as they did not know any better. There was a carryover of destructive entitlement from one family to another or from one generation to the next. Thus, the legacy lived on.

COMPASSION

Although I point out negative patterns of behavior on the part of parents and the resultant carryovers in their child/children, this is done chiefly for analysis and understanding of a family situation, not to place blame.

I believe compassion is a very important aspect of being a therapist. When we look at George's mother (Chapter 5), my reaction as the child's therapist was one of initial irritation and frustration. But George's mother was an unhappy woman who had tragically lost both her mother and her husband—her mother to a horrible accidental death and her husband to the prison system for his outrageous bursts of anger and behavior. To help George, I realized that I had to be compassionate about his mother and explain her issues, so that George would accept and understand his mother as she really was. Then he could move on with his own growth and wellness. In some ways this book is a request for compassion for those who do not seem to "fit in" with other people.

In discussing madness Jules Henry (1965/1971) says, "I perceive these families as Greek tragedies without gods. They seem destined to misery and even catastrophe because they are locked in by their past and by configurations of love, hate, anxiety, and shame, which became established in the home, rigid as the walls" (p. xx). This is true of dysfunctional scapegoating families as well in which one person is chosen to bear the brunt of the family's anger and pain. How do we understand relational aspects and the resources of these families? If we put together the past history of the parents (as children in their own families of origin) and the constellation of personal relations established in their families of procreation, largely through the couple's relationship and their parental relationship with the children, we have a conception of family history. So what has happened with these families is that the threads of behavior patterns from their own original family cultures have been woven into their present lives. The quality of life in these families is born out of their own re-creation of what they have taken from their original family cultures without being aware of it. Among these people I observed a helplessness about changing their own destiny, for they do not know how to change.

Let us be compassionate for a moment and look at the different situations of the scapegoated child and his or her parents. Learning to live with a person you do not love or respect and learning to live with a person you know does not love or respect you is like learning not to live (Henry, 1965–1971). It requires learning to talk in frightened whispers; how to deny what you feel; how to hate without showing it; how to weep without tears; and how to hide that the shame you are living in is your family reality.

This brings to mind Emma (Chapter 5), who lived at home playing the mother's conspiring partner and knowing that her father hated her. Emma hated him in return, quietly and desperately. Often, in such families, there is no foundation for a loving relationship with the children, as the parents themselves are emotionally deprived and do not know how to cope with their children.

How are these individuals deprived? Their deprivation is a reflection of how they have been treated and how they have learned to treat others. I believe no person learns to feel in a simple way simply because no love is open, direct, and simple. One learns to love in association with a parent or caretaker who has his or her own unique way of expressing love and wanting it. When a child grows up in a home, he or she will understand, feel, and want love as he or she has learned it—through give and take, manipulation, acting-out behaviors, or playing the savior of the family. Therefore, I found what goes along with growing up, be it violence or physical or emotional abuse, is not some intruding, unconscious behavior but that which was learned. I have reached the conclusion that family contexts are historical; they express their own time and culture.

Again, when we look at family life, we know that no one trains an adult to think in terms of enriching his or her family life, yet people are instructed how to avoid failure and how to be successful in a career. I wonder how families manage to survive, because they do survive.

HOW THIS BOOK IS WRITTEN

This book is not free of jargon, though I originally intended to keep the language simple. It was difficult to use everyday language because I needed to present complex psychoanalytic terms, and systemic and psychodynamic interpretations. In retrospect, I do not regret my choice of specialized language, mostly in my interpretations, as it is necessary to understand severe scapegoating and thereby help readers in their own personal and/or professional battles in such situations. As the reader will note, analyzing scapegoated individuals involves a complex interweaving of values, people, emotions, and actions.

RATIONALE FOR THIS BOOK

My interest in scapegoating started while I researched material for *Pathways to Family Myths* (Pillari, 1986) and worked on the concept of scapegoating. The fact that one individual could be "all bad, negative, or useless" and be a burden bearer was mind-boggling. I saw scapegoated people in therapy much too often, some mildly scapegoated and others severely. What happens when one recognizes another as a scapegoat? Can we go beyond scapegoating to help these people survive and value themselves? This sparked my interest in writing about them. This book provides therapeutic information to those who deal with scapegoating. I also hope that adults who read this book will avoid mistakes with their own children, as they understand the tedious journey scapegoating follows through parent- or caretaker-child relationships and, sometimes, through generations.

In this book the emphasis is mostly on children and on adults who were scapegoated as children. The cases used are mostly cases that I have handled. I wish I could thank the client organizations by name, but I do not wish to violate privacy. The names and identifying data of the cases have, of course, been disguised. I am grateful to those families and individuals who served as models in presenting scapegoat situations.

Scapegoating in Families

*Intergenerational Patterns of
Physical and Emotional Abuse*

1

The Nature of Scapegoating

Laura walked into the gloomy living room, where her mother and father were involved in an intense argument about family expenses. It seemed like a "who can scream louder" contest. When the mother saw Laura, she withdrew from the argument and exclaimed in an exasperated tone of voice, "Where have you been? You have not done any of your chores, and with your ugly face, whom could you be spending your time with?"

Laura, barely 16, looked at her mother in anger and disbelief and screamed, "I hate you; I hate the way you yell at me!" and ran out of the room. Mother looked at Father and said, "There she goes again. Call her back and ask her where she's been all this time." At the mother's insistence, the father yelled, "Don't talk to your mother like that. Come back here at once and tell us where you have been." There was no response, so the father continued, "You're grounded if you don't tell us at once." Mother was still angry. The discussion then turned to how to deal with Laura, who was "such a miserable child."

Laura is the family scapegoat. Her family has a number
of problems, ranging from financial difficulties to a lack
of meaningful communication among its members, particularly between husband and wife. Yet all these problems
are set aside when Laura walks into the home. The couple
take enough time away from their heated discussion to
blame Laura for all their misery. She is viewed as the
cause of unhappiness in this family.

The family scapegoat is the burden bearer and is unfairly
blamed for problems in the family; the scapegoated person
as a member of the family system takes on some degree
of responsibility for these problems, too. The role is a
prejudicial role, but one the scapegoat accepts and supports (Sieburg, 1985). Every member of the family, including the scapegoat, acts to maintain the family system's
homeostatic balance at the expense of one element of the
system (Sieburg, 1985).

WHAT IS SCAPEGOATING?

The idea of scapegoating is as old as society itself. Frazer
(1922), in *The Golden Bough*, records that scapegoating goes
back to antiquity, when people practiced public scapegoating. People or animals were sacrificed for the well-
being of the rest of society. Frazer represents scapegoating
as a process in which evil forces are embodied in a visible
form or loaded upon a specific material medium, which
act as vehicles to carry off the evil. The scapegoat's function
is to effect a total clearance of all ills that have been
infesting a group of people.

In classical Rome, every year on the Ides of March, a
man clad in skins was led in procession through the streets,
beaten with long white rods, and driven out of the city.

This person was called Mamurius Veturius, "old Mars," and the ceremony took place on the day preceding the first full moon of the old Roman year (which began on the first of March). This skin-clad man must have represented Mars of the past year, who was driven out at the beginning of the "first full moon of the new Roman year" (Frazer, 1920). The notion that a group of people can transfer their guilt and sufferings to another being who then carries their burdens was also common in other ancient cultures.

In an ancient Hindu ritual the pangs of thirst could be transferred from one sick person to another. The operator seats the pair on branches, back to back, the sufferer with his face to the East and the healthy man with his face to the West. In this manner the operator transfers the pangs of thirst from the thirsty soul to the other soul, who obligingly receives them in his stead (Frazer, 1920).

The World Book Encyclopedia (1988) entry by Gary G. Porton states,

> Scapegoat originally meant one of the two goats received by the Jewish High Priest in ancient Jerusalem on the Day of Atonement. One was for Jehovah, the Hebrew God, and was killed as a sacrificial offering. The second was called the scapegoat. This one was for Azazel, which may have been the spirit of evil. The priest laid his hands on the scapegoat as he confessed the peoples' sins. Then the priest sent the scapegoat into the wilderness. This was a symbol that the sins had been put away, or forgiven.
>
> Today, when someone refers to a person as a scapegoat, it means he has been made to take the

blame for something which is the fault of another
(p. 172).

The Family Scapegoat

The use of scapegoating for the benefit of a group of
people was a way of life in some civilizations. In the same
way, it is not uncommon for families to utilize a single
member as a scapegoat to maintain the coherence of the
family (Pillari, 1986). The projection of hostilities to the
outside via a scapegoat helps some groups achieve unity.
The scapegoated individual in this family performs the
important function of channeling family tensions and
providing the family with a basis of solidarity.

In some families children are brought into the world to
"bind" the family unit, "to keep the family together." Many
couples are in conflict before children are born, and they
hope that children will help the marriage. When the
conflicts do not disappear, the couple stay together "for
the sake of the children." The resentment they have toward
each other may be transferred to the children.

Do children wish to live for the sake of the parents? It
depends. Most of the time, if the child has *not* been
scapegoated, he or she is likely to feel a strong need to
get away from the family conflict and family pathology.
One person mentioned that he wished his parents had
divorced because all he faced when he lived with them
was strife and pain. Fortunately, this child was not the
family scapegoat and was able to view the family situation
somewhat objectively. The scapegoated child, especially if
the scapegoating has been a lifelong pattern, will probably
feel responsible for all the family pain and want to stay
physically and/or emotionally in order to make amends.

Simon, Stierlin, and Wynne (1985) note that, as applied to family theory and therapy, this classical metaphor of scapegoat refers to situations in which parents attempt to resolve a conflict between themselves by seeing or exaggerating problems in another individual. Usually such a person is "chosen" or recruited to be the scapegoat. A scapegoat is ideally a person who is weaker and smaller, at least in mental stature. Therefore, the easiest target for this type of oppression is a young person—normally a child in the family.

Parents project their interpersonal tensions and conflicts upon one of the children in order to bring about harmony in their troubled marital relationship. The child is then triangulated into a position of being the burden bearer, and a detouring of conflicts results. Triangulation refers to the expansion of a conflict-ridden, dyadic relationship to include a third individual. This results in diffusion or cover-up of the conflict. When couples are faced with the dilemma that one of them could win and the other lose, or when they are afraid that their relationship will not last, the solution to the dilemma may be to include a third person. The parent who constantly loses may compensate for defeat by entering into an overt or covert bond with a third party and thereby reestablish the balance of the dyadic relationship; this becomes the perverse triangle. Conflict between a couple is diverted when a child (the scapegoat) provides a problem or is delegated to produce problematic behavior (Simon, Stierlin, & Wynne, 1985). This concept will be further discussed under "Triangulation."

If the child is viewed as a passive victim and the parents as the guilty parties, the road leading to the creation of constructive relationships is almost nonexistent. Family relationships are cyclical, and multidirectional ways exist by which families cope with and adapt to their own problems. How can a child be triangulated? If one family member gets another member to act crazy or wild or to be a troublemaker, then the first person disowns his or her own craziness, wildness, or troublesome behavior. By a similar mechanism of projection, adult family members' behavior can sometimes predict their own pathology; in order to avoid dealing with their problem they may unconsciously or subconsciously select and identify a "crazy" child and use this child as the family scapegoat.

Family Interaction

Scapegoating, more than any other relational pathology seen in families, is usually well explained by viewing the family as a system. The notion of the family as a "system" has its beginnings in the general systems theory that was pioneered by Ludwig von Bertalanffy (1934). Von Bertalanffy's early work in the biological sciences saw the essential phenomena of life as individual entities called "organisms." According to von Bertalanffy (1968) an organism is composed of mutually dependent parts and processes that stand in mutual interaction.

One can begin to define a family system by paraphrasing Von Bertalanffy: an order of people with their intellectual, emotional, and behavioral processes that stand in mutual interaction. This family system has many ways and styles of exchanging matter and energy with its environment, including the distinctive human ability for imagining that an exchange has taken place when in reality it has not. The system normally has self-regulating capacities, which include moral, political, social, religious, economic, and idiosyncratic values and constraints. In addition, it is intrinsically active, that is, one does not have to look outside the family system to understand a sudden shift in family dynamics (Okun & Rappaport, 1980).

Kerr and Bowen (1988) indicate that the emotionally determined functioning of the family members generates a family emotional "atmosphere" or "field," and this in turn influences the emotional functioning of each person. The result is the production of an emotionally driven relationship system that is present in all families. The intensity of the emotional process may vary from family to family, and within the same family system over time, but it is always present to some degree. This emotional process in the family system results in members occupying different functioning positions in the family. A person's functioning in the family has an important influence on his or her beliefs, values, attitudes, feelings, and behavior.

Another important aspect of the family functioning system is that the members operate in reciprocal relationships to one another. A young child shapes the behavior of an older sibling, as much as an older child shapes the behavior of a younger one. To say this another way, an "overfunctioning" person shapes the attitudes, feelings, and behavior of an "underfunctioning" person, as much as the underfunctioning person shapes the attitudes, feelings, and behavior of an overfunctioning person.

Beside feelings, beliefs, and attitudes, reciprocal functioning is important and evident in creating and maintaining the various functioning positions in the family system. In the homes of scapegoated children, repetitive patterns of action commonly occur not because of one person's sickness or internal conflicts, but because patterns are useful for the functionality of the whole family system. If the needed role of scapegoat is not played by one member, then it must be assumed by another. Nathan Ackerman noted this type of family interdependence when he treated a family with a psychotic daughter. Ackerman writes:

> While treating a family with an only daughter—
> a girl of sixteen years with an early and labile
> form of psychotic disorder—it struck me forcibly
> as I watched the family, and also as I viewed over
> and over the film record of these interviews, that
> when one part of the family came to life, the
> other part seemed to die. I am talking now of
> the sheer flow of affect, not words. The quality
> of coming back to life, affectively speaking,
> seemed to swing back and forth, pendulum-
> fashion, from the parents to the daughter and
> back again. As I studied the process, it became
> plain that this was a consistent and repetitive
> pattern. If the young psychotic girl showed signs
> of life, the parents literally lay down and died
> before my eyes; if the parents became vocal and
> excited, the girl faded away. One part of the
> family seemed to draw the breath of life at the
> expense of the other (Ackerman, 1966, p. 79).

Not all scapegoating lends itself to understanding the dynamics of the family system. However, in most disturbed families a particular child becomes involved in tensions existing between parents, though other children may also get into peripheral trouble with the parents, off and on. In families who are fairly well adjusted, the tensions are handled in such a manner that the children do not become pathologically involved. However, when some parents have serious issues to work on, and there are a number of severe conflicts that have not been resolved, a child is recruited to be the "problem." The parents feel themselves to be at opposite poles, so that one spouse act outs one side of the conflict, the other spouse act outs the other side, and the child is represented as an important aspect of their disagreement. In some situations of intense discord, husband and wife develop an equilibrium in which they minimize contact with one another and minimize expressions of affect, making it possible for them to live together. But this equilibrium involves many difficulties. For instance,

> Fourteen-year-old Joy is caught in her parents' marital problems. For the sake of the children, the couple decided to live together in icy silence. Not showing overt anger was an accepted phenomenon in this family. Joy was her mother's confidante, which meant going out with her mother, running errands for her, and occasionally missing school, if her mother needed her at home. The father, in turn, expected Joy's help in household chores, which included taking care of his laundry. Joy is overburdened with family responsibilities. However, if anything goes wrong in the family routine, Joy is quickly blamed for it. She is still a child and more vulnerable than an adult. Thus one of the serious problems of this family's equilibrium is the scapegoating of the child.

SOURCES OF TENSION THAT
LEAD TO SCAPEGOATING

Some couples have deep fears about their marriages and about the behavior of their partners. One young woman could not predict how her husband would respond to her behavior, yet the type of response that the husband gave was very important to this woman, though it was thought to be potentially damaging. The greatest tragedy in this situation is that both partners felt they could not deal with the situation directly because they considered direct communication very dangerous. Therefore, they resorted to manipulations, masking, and evasions. Tensions arose because of the personality patterns of each of the spouses.

Nina was angry with her husband, John, for subtly insulting her when she was with her friends. She also cares about his opinion. So when John returns home from work, she gets back at him by telling the children to do something that he does not like. She asks them to take their toys to the garage and play there. When John comes home, he beeps his horn and yells at the children to get away from the garage. He is particularly mad at 4-year-old Otto, for he considers him to be a troublemaker. Then Nina slowly walks into the situation; she is happy because she successfully upset her husband, and he is aware that she allowed the children to play in the garage. Nina subtly got back at her husband for making insulting provocations in front of her friends and now John would feel undermined by her. However, she readily agrees with him that Otto was the troublemaker.

In this family the person chosen to break tensions between the couple is Otto, and he is scapegoated frequently.

Cultural-Value Orientation

People bring different values from their families of origin into marriage. Sometimes when members of two diverse ethnic groups are joined together, there are more areas open to conflict, particularly when one of the partners has difficulty understanding or accepting the other's ways. When marriage partners have been socialized into different patterns, they may be working on different assumptions. Many families seen in therapy have problems of this kind. Some individuals try to shift quickly to a different pattern that they have not really internalized, and others try to live with their conflicting orientations.

Thus, when husband and wife come from very different family backgrounds, or when marriage takes place for the wrong reasons (for example, a pregnancy, peer pressure, or to escape from a conflicted home), the solidarity of the marriage may become questionable. Tensions and conflicts also occur when people of different levels of self-esteem marry. When both partners have low-esteem, there is an increased likelihood that problems will arise in the marital situation (Pillari, 1986). Couples with low self-esteem are also less individuated and look to one another for complete happiness and end up in enmeshed patterns.

Difficulties that arise out of cultural-value conflicts are sometimes centered in the problems of individual performance. Often, there is a pull toward American middle-class achievement patterns. Families who have partially internalized American middle-class values and the values of their own ethnic family system may find it impossible to live up to both sets of values. When there is no compromise and the family chooses one set of values over another, the result is conflict.

> Forty-year-old Sharon and her husband Paul had been married for 15 years. Sharon came from a permissive and democratic family culture, whereas Paul was from a conservative family. At the time of their marriage, Paul was everything Sharon wanted, at least in terms of economic provision and social status. Paul was also very conservative and set rules about how things should be done. As time passed, however, Sharon found that Paul was a domineering man with a bad temper. Despite their differences, the couple were afraid to let go of each other.
>
> When family tensions began to overwhelm them, they decided to have a baby, thinking that the baby would improve matters. One child did not clear up their problems, and with aspiring zeal, they ended up with four children and a large number of family tensions and conflicts. The children took sides with the parents about who was right and who was wrong. The oldest child, Paula, had participated in this process for a long time. As the first child of her parents, Paula was the chosen victim and was put into situations where she could not win; and added to that burden, her parents constantly found fault with her. At the age of 14, Paula was not allowed

to go out with her friends because Sharon and Paul were afraid that she would become promiscuous, even though she was not dating anyone.

The scapegoating had started when Paula was an infant. As she grew older, Paula became aware of the various patterns of conflict in the family and took on the role of scapegoat willingly—as she wanted her parents to remain married. As an adult, Paula continued to take on roles that caused her pain, stress, and anxiety. As one therapist mentioned, "I am always amazed at how fairly successful adults, long separated from family dynamics, still live out the myth of the "scapegoating role"—often in work settings, relationships, and even in religious practice settings."

Skewed and Schismatic Families

According to the Lidz group, there are two types of families that are more prone to dysfunctions. Based on their research in New Haven in the 1950s, the Lidz group (Lidz, Fleck, & Cornelison, 1958) studied families of schizophrenics. They explicated two patterns of marital relationships which they labelled *skewed* and *schismatic*. Such families reveal disturbances in the parents' marital relationship. In the skewed family, marital relations are characterized by a strong partner, usually the mother, and a weak partner, usually the father, who accepts the domination and does not attempt to resist it. In the schismatic family, the marital relationship is characterized by chronic hostility and mutual withdrawal. The marriage is filled with persecutions and there is no common purpose or reciprocity of roles in the skewed and schismatic families. Each partner takes on a rigid, inflexible, stereotypical role and is unable to respond to the changing needs of other family members. The tensions created in this marital situation can lead to problems among children who are caught in the rigidity of parental roles, under which lie the children's feelings of anger and fear and result in confusion or even pathology. Such troubled children become the center of attention in a negative way, and later on they take on the role scapegoat.

Andrea gave birth to Nick while married to Tom, whom she claimed she did not love. However Nick was not her husband's child but the child of her lover, Richard, with whom she had been involved briefly; and she claimed she did not really love Richard either. Later she divorced Tom and married Peter. Neither Peter nor Nick knew that Nick's father was not her first husband, Tom; Andrea kept this information to herself.

Andrea and Peter developed grave marital problems and Nick, intensely disliked by his mother, was scapegoated in this situation. Nick visited Richard about once a year, but he did not know that this man was his "real dad." Nick assumed that he was visiting an uncle, a fabrication kept up by his mother. When Nick was 13, the scapegoating took a turn for the worse: Andrea's second marriage was crumbling. He heard the silent message "Rescue us," and accordingly Nick started to act out by getting into trouble at school and at home.

Amid all this commotion and pain in the family,

10-year-old Donna, the child of Peter and Andrea, was viewed as the "good child." She did
very well in her role, as did her older, 13-year-
old scapegoated brother, Nick, who was the "bad
child." Donna had no friends and never showed
any affect during family therapy sessions, yet the
parents continuously claimed that she was a "won-
derful child." Donna was the exalted one and the
family's darling, and she always had her way. She
instructed herself to dissolve into tears or to take
the disposition of a martyr, whichever action
suited the situation. This behavior kept her out
of trouble with her parents. Nick was the one
who had to be "fixed," even though he was the
one who had been at a disadvantage all his life
and continued to be the recipient of the family
anger and pain.

In the family, there were two sets of rules, one set for
Nick and the other for his sister. Donna could go out and
play, but Nick was not given this privilege. The two sets
of rules created double standards in the family. This
bothered Nick, who responded by acting out. When he
acted out he was viewed as the "bad" kid and was subject
to even more restrictions. His parents spent a great deal
of time trying to "correct" Nick's behavior, and this helped
to maintain the family homeostasis.

Triangulation

Bowen (1976) states that an "automatic emotional response system" involves at least two people. When there
is less tension, most two-parent systems operate in a fairly

calm and stable manner. However, when there is a great deal of tension and anxiety and the couple cannot manage it, a third person is usually "triangulated" in order to reduce the tension. The most vulnerable person, usually a child, will be used in this manner. Children are less self-differentiated, more vulnerable, and also more likely to be seduced by the emotions of a highly tense two-person system, namely the parents. This leads to triangulation of a child. Triangulation leaves the individual disabled long after the triangle has been broken.

Minuchin (1974) describes the different forms of pathological triangle structures under the concept of a rigid triad. In triangulation, overtly or covertly conflicted parents attempt to win the sympathy and support of a child at the cost of their spouse's relationship to the child. This places the child in an intense conflict of loyalty, which Minuchin calls a detouring of conflicts, scapegoating, and triangulation of the child.

When the tension becomes too high for dissipation through a single triangle, other people can be triangulated, and thus there is a potential for a series of extending, interlocking triangles. Moreover, when all available family members have been triangulated, the family reaches outside of itself to the extended family, to the neighborhood, and finally to the police and other social welfare agencies (Bowen, 1976).

The fusion that the child develops with the emotional system of the family inhibits and prevents his or her normal process of differentiation of intellect and emotion. Any growth that threatens to move the child out of the triangle is viewed as a threat to the family's homeostasis. As a result, this person's differentiation of self is retarded and subordinated to the family system's needs in order to maintain its present level of functioning.

What is differentiation of self? According to Bowen (1976) there are levels of differentiation of self. Bowen sees individual and system maturity as hinging on the degree of fusion or differentiation achieved between the intellect and emotionality. People with low levels of differentiation are unable to separate their thoughts and feelings from their families of origin, whereas people who have high levels of differentiation are able to function effectively and are able to make judgments and decisions independent of their families of origin.

Bowen classifies the differentiation of self into four categories. People at the lowest level of differentiation are fused with the family ego mass in such a way that they are constantly vulnerable to any family dilemma. Their emotional and intellectual fusion with the undifferentiated family ego mass makes them totally relationship oriented, and they devote a great deal of energy and time to seeking love and approval as well as validation. Higher degrees of differentiation allow for better integration of the individual within the family emotional relationship, making possible within the individual a higher degree of differentiation between intellect and emotion.

In families that have lower degrees of differentiation, there is anxiety and concern about the prevailing stress in the family, which is present in the form of chronic anxiety. Chronic anxiety in the system results in scapegoating, and with it, as a painful bonus, there is symptom formation, dysfunction, and illness.

Whatever the problem, the scapegoated person, together with the rest of the family, maintains the homeostasis of the family, though the homeostasis may mean misery and anguish. Such families are usually enmeshed and would rather be in pain and together rather than disintegrate.

THE SELECTION OF THE SCAPEGOAT

Factors

Factors that are crucial to the scapegoating role are unresolved tensions in the family, which may be so serious that they cannot be contained without a discharge. One very common way to discharge them is to find an appropriate person to symbolize them. In the cases presented in this book, the chosen person was the most vulnerable and thus the one who became the scapegoat. For families with a large number of problems, it is not easy to scapegoat an outsider, especially when the parents have internalized the standards of the external community and thus have great difficulty in finding a legitimate basis for scapegoating outsiders. Even if family members experience strong feelings of antagonism toward outsiders, they rarely express their antagonism directly; instead they bring it home and unconsciously or subconsciously use it against the vulnerable child who is the family scapegoat.

However, in some families, outsiders are not entirely overlooked. In these situations, parents blame outsiders such as their employers, teachers, neighbors, "white people" or "black people" for their troubles and weaknesses and thus form interlocking triangles with the outside world; a single triangle or multiple triangles with a scapegoated child or children is not sufficient to absorb all of the family tensions and anxieties.

However, the tensions in such families do not necessarily lead to difficulties with the outside world. Frequently, the latent hostilities between husband and wife make it very difficult for the individuals to deal with their problems and with each other directly and openly. There is always the danger that one of the partners may become extremely angry and vindictive. All these factors may converge on a child as the most appropriate individual on whom to discharge family tensions. Why does this happen? First, the child is in a relatively powerless position in comparison to the parents. Second, the young person is in a dependent position, unable to leave the family or to challenge the parents' superior authority (Vogel & Bell, 1981).

As Sieburg (1985) observes, the selection of a child as a scapegoat is largely an unconscious process. However, the choice is based on certain characteristics of the child that mark him or her as being different from the rest of the family. For instance, one scapegoated child was considered by his family to be effeminate. The differences that mark a child for selection are not random. They are significant in terms of their symbolic relation to the real source of tension in the family. For example, if the parents' unexpressed conflict involves the husband's lack of success, the child who is an underachiever in his studies is a natural target for scapegoating; the academic failure mirrors the father's professional position. In reality the father's failure may go unacknowledged, but the mother's constant criticism of the child is an expression of her dissatisfaction with her husband's economic or occupational status, an attitude that she cannot express. Once the child is scapegoated, he or she easily becomes the burden bearer for the family's other problems.

Other factors that may influence the selection of the scapegoat are the sex and ordinal position of the child in the family. If either one or both parents had unpleasant experiences with their sisters in their own families of origin, the scapegoated person might be a female child; if they had problems with an older sibling, the couple might choose an older child for scapegoating. The child who is chosen, usually unconsciously, may have a low IQ, suffer from physical abnormalities, or be unattractive, giving the parents an excuse to say that they do not deserve such a child and therefore nothing is wrong in treating the child differently. This leads to role assignment for the child. For instance, in some alcoholic families, the child who is scapegoated is generally shy, unassertive, and overly sensitive.

Role Assignment

Once selected as the family scapegoat, the child is expected to be a "problem child." As mentioned previously, this child helps to release family tensions that arise from other sources. The dynamics are generally quite clear: the child is also "trained" to be extremely sensitive to rising tensions and anxieties and, in response, to act out or to misbehave, or to play the role of the perfect child, in order to direct the attention toward himself or herself. By acting out, the child distracts the family from its other tensions and successfully diverts to himself or herself the pain and anger that is felt in the family. The child's behavior appears to reduce the anxiety she or he feels when the system is out of balance. This child becomes so well aware of the family's tensions that he or she will repeat the misbehavior as long it serves the purpose of reducing tensions in the family. Thus, such a child develops a functional role to play in maintaining the family's homeostasis.

The role that is given or taken by a member of the family is closely tied to that person's sense of identity. Roles are organized, and they tell us who we are, how we are, and how others can act towards us. Families may give members nicknames or pet names, which stand for myths that are present in the families and which place family members in different slots. One child may be described as the "golden child," another as the "family worrier" or "the ugly one." Role creation in the family even when a child is young is an extremely complex process and involves interactions among members, intrapsychic experiences within family members, multigenerational legacies (Karpel & Strauss, 1983), and social contexts.

Why do parents who are supposed to be caring and loving towards their children scapegoat them? Usually, the parents' defenses are brittle but they are much stronger than children's defenses. Because the child's personality is still forming, he or she can be molded to assume a particular role that the family assigns. When the child takes on qualities that are disliked in one or both parents, or qualities of a disliked family-of-origin member, this child symbolically becomes the person on whom the parents' own anxieties can be focused. The scapegoated person develops severe tensions and is unable to perform the usual developmental tasks, but continues to perform essential, irreplaceable functions for the family. In some ways, the degree of pain and dysfunction for the child is relatively low compared with the functional gains for this family, at least in the short run.

As mentioned before, the scapegoated child may have a physical defect or be unattractive. If problems arise, it is this child who becomes the focus. The child is viewed as a punishment from some supernatural being for the family's failure to live up to its ideals or to live up to some internal family value, such as marital fidelity. The malformed child may also be seen as the result of parents' sins. In such situations, the child might take on the problems of the family and be maltreated.

Larry's mother, Sylvia, had a long, unhappy marriage during which she bore 11 children. Out of the 11 children, this mother picked on one child, Larry, who had an unusually large, dark birthmark on his face; Larry was also squint-eyed and resembled her abusive husband, Frank. She treated him with anger and negligence. One day, Frank had a serious fight with Sylvia in which he used an iron rod to hurt her and then left home. Although Sylvia was happy to see him go, she panicked about the children and the means for providing for them.

During that time, her anger against Larry appeared to be reaching unprecedented heights. One ominous day, in a fit of temper, she pulled his hand and stuck it into a flame on the stove. Sylvia's complaint was that Larry was a bad, extremely troublesome child, and he needed the punishment to put him in his place. The abuse that Larry suffered was considered serious and required his temporary placement in a foster home. Sylvia fought for him and took him back, but continued to treat him as if he were the cause of all family problems. So after a number of foster care placements, Larry was placed in a residential setting where his remonstrative acting out and abusive behavior, in turn, reached tremendous heights. Ironically, Sylvia considered most of her other 10 children as being fairly "decent kids."

When couples have problems in their married lives, they may pretend that these problems do not exist. But as time passes, they become more and more aware of each other's defects and become polarized towards each other due to their conflicts. Each parent represents one side of the polarization, what Helm Stierlin (1973) has termed a "cat-dog" marriage (marriage of opposites); unhappy with their tensions and anxieties, these couples still cannot live without each other. One such couple appeared to have a number of problems, and all their anger, tension, and pain were displaced onto their eldest child, who was considered to be the most easily available. Often, once assigned, the scapegoat role becomes the child's permanent role in the family. However, some children get away from the assigned role when they leave home. When this happens in families with tremendous tensions, the next available child is used for scapegoating to diffuse the marital conflicts of the couple.

Kerry, the eldest in a family of four children, was the designated scapegoat. Every problem that the family had was displaced onto him, making him the most victimized person in the family. For example, one younger sister had power and control over him and the rest of the siblings. Whatever Kerry did was considered to be "no good." To make matters worse, there were always fights and quarrels between the parents. Often the father believed that Kerry was the reason for these problems. Kerry had been taken to numerous therapists to be "fixed," but the treatments never seemed to work. In therapy, Kerry mentioned that he would return home with the idea of behaving really well, but when conflict arose between family members, he was caught up in these quickly. Before long, he was blamed for every single problem in the family.

In high school Kerry met a fine girl and they fell in love. He spent less and less time at home, and his grades began to improve. As if an alarm clock had gone off, the younger brother, who until then had been the designated "good kid," started to act out and to get into trouble at school as well as at home. The younger brother "heard" the unconscious message and became the designated second scapegoat of the family, bearing the problems of the family as Kerry had done before him.

As indicated earlier in this chapter, the scapegoat is not necessarily an innocent victim. Although the role is negative, it is supportively played by the scapegoat to help maintain the status quo of the family—even though this status quo is unhealthy.

INDUCTION INTO THE SCAPEGOAT ROLE

It is important to remember that in families where children have been inducted into the role of scapegoat, there will be a certain degree of family disturbance. Evasion and denial of real feelings and exploitation of the child or children, can exist.

To be induced to play the role of scapegoat, the child must be a willing sacrifice for the family. Let's look at 15-year-old Jerry.

Jerry was the family scapegoat and his induction took place when he was very young. He remembered that when he was five years old, his parents had a serious fight and his mother, Cheryl, decided that she did not wish to live. Filled with oppressive depression, she locked herself in a bathroom and cut her wrist with a knife. Her husband, Arnold, could not rescue her, as the bathroom door was locked. So he broke the glass window of the bathroom and instead of going in by himself, he sent Jerry through the window with the order that he persuade his mother not to kill herself. Five-year-old Jerry was shocked to see his mother in a pool of blood, but he took the additional responsibility and persuaded her not to kill herself. Thus began his induction in an extremely overt fashion.

To be successful as the scapegoat, the child must carry on the role irrespective of the pain, hostility, and anxieties experienced in connection with the role. In order to be inducted into the role, the child has to receive messages, usually implicit messages from the adult members. The parents are usually inconsistent in their messages, their explicit messages contradicting the implicit ones, and this adds to the child's confusion and sense of being pulled in different directions.

Inconsistency

Inconsistency is the most common means of inducting a child into the role of scapegoat. The most common form of inconsistency is the manner in which the child was implicitly or explicitly introduced into the role. On the basis of this explicit or implicit role assignment, the child acts out, either at home in school, or in both, expressing the hostility and uncooperativeness that affect the child's relationship with the outside world (Vogel & Bell, 1981).

> Paul was taken out of school because he tried to choke a younger boy until the boy had turned blue. When the school authorities questioned him, Paul burst out laughing, saying that he was only playing around with this kid, who did not know how to fight back. Somehow there appeared to be no connection between the facts of the incident and the nature of Paul's true feelings. Initially Paul appeared to be afraid of authority, but it became evident that he was experiencing a great deal of anxiety and pain, which he turned into laughter. His laughter could have been his form of defense against anxiety. In Malan's (1979) phrase, this reaction could be called the defense of superficiality. Paul was afraid to examine his feelings about what the choking might really have done to the young boy.
>
> Later, Paul's parents were summoned to the school, and everyone reported to the principal's office. After due discussion, Paul was suspended and his parents were requested to take him home. Although the parents appeared upset and angry in front of the principal, as soon as they were out of the office, the mother giggled like a schoolgirl and said, "What's wrong with playing around a little bit? Paul is a child, too." With this statement,

the seriousness of the punishment was dismissed and Paul was given subtle permission to express feelings of aggression at school. This was explicit support of his behavior, which had been specifically condemned by the school authorities.

Thus, in some situations, double messages help to induct the child into a role that parents are eager for the child to play. This kind of outcome can accelerate the child's role as a troublemaker in school and at home and unwittingly, he or she may become or continue to be the chosen scapegoated child in the family.

Children who are resistant to parental orders or express aggression towards siblings also receive double messages. The parents may criticize the child for "bad behavior," and at times may even administer punishment, but at the same time they may implicitly support the same behavior that they appear to condemn.

> For example, a mother asks her 10-year-old daughter, Marla, to discipline her younger brothers when she (the mother) is away from home. Marla does what she witnessed at home—when Albert cries, she beats him just like her mother. However, when the mother returns home, she gets angry with Marla for beating Albert. Two days later she punishes Marla excessively for beating Albert. This incident was precipitated when Marla disobeyed her mother. A few days later when the mother is upset with Albert because he is troubling her, she asks Marla to get him out of her sight and beat him, if necessary.

How do parents subtly encourage their children? According to Vogel and Bell (1981) there are several ways. One is not following through on the threats of punishment. Another is delayed punishment. They may show indifference to and acceptance of the negative behavior, saying, in effect, "That's just the way, Johnny is." They may take an unusual interest in the child's symptom, gaining the child considerable secondary gratification. Another form of parenting is love without boundaries. The parents do not set any limits on what the child is allowed to say, do, or hear. Later on, such a child gets into trouble at home and in the outside world when he or she acts irresponsibly and does not respect authority. Also some parents may exempt children from certain responsibilities that are crucial for the child's well-being.

> For instance, Christopher complained that he had too much homework to do. Instead of encouraging him to complete it, his mother told him that it was all right not to complete it, because the teacher was stupid to give such a heavy load to a young kid. However, when Christopher came home at the end of the semester with a poor report card, the mother was amazed that Christopher was such a poor student. She became angry at his performance and called him a "stupid, good-for-nothing kid." The child was confused by the inconsistency in which he had been caught.

Another destructive form of inconsistency that traps a child in the scapegoat role occurs when one parent encourages one kind of behavior and the other parent discourages it. Thus, the child is caught in the conflicts of the parents. In the midst of this dilemma, the child must also face the parents' hostilities toward each other, which are redirected towards the child. Although this release spares the partners the agony of telling each other off, it is the young child who bears the pain, which causes him or her a tremendous amount of strain. When the parental attitude toward a particular behavior is implicit, the parents are free to deny any direct involvement in it. However, if they are aware of their opposition, they may be afraid to confront each other, and therefore all the hostility is directed toward the child, who continues to be the victim in such cases (Lederer & Jackson, 1968).

Sometimes a parent's encouragement of a particular behavior in the child is so subtle that the other parent will not find it obvious enough to criticize the child. A delicate antagonistic balance results with the child in the middle.

Expectations

Expectations are a means of inducting a person into a scapegoated role. In some families both parents convey to the child implicit and explicit expectations that are subtly different. A child's behavior may at one time be criticized for being very negative and meet with heavy punishments. At another time the same behavior may be ignored and or even implicitly encouraged by the parents' supportive and affectionate manner. The parents might rationalize their inconsistency and implicit expectations by saying that they do not wish to be harsh to their child. However, the end result helps the child to preserve the disliked behavior.

> For instance, one child was constantly tempted to take cookies from a cookie jar and overeat. This desire led to a weight problem. The parents

were encouraged to keep the cookie jar out of
the child's reach, and both were asked to give the
same message that cookies were not really good
for the child but that he would get one or two
every evening. The parents refused to ban cookies
in the house because they both liked to eat cookies.
With both parents consistent in their messages,
the child stopped asking for cookies and did not
go looking for them. When it appeared that this
problem had been worked through, the mother
bought an attractive cookie jar and left it on the
kitchen table within easy reach of the child. The
temptation was too much for the child, who
opened it and ate the cookies.

It appeared that the parents had consciously disap-
proved of the child's eating cookies but had implicitly
encouraged him. The implicit demands upon the child
seemed more powerful than the explicit ones, for the
attractive cookie jar and cookies were within reach of the
child and gave him all the messages he wished to hear.
One might predict that as the child gets older the sanctions
for him to eat the cookies that are not good for him would
increase, and as problems in the family become more
intense, he would be picked on to play the role into which
he had already been inducted (Vogel & Bell, 1981).

When conflicting expectations coexist for a long period
of time, it is likely to internalize the conflict. Once a child
has been inducted as a scapegoat, an escalating spiral is
created to perpetuate the child's role assignment. As soon
as the child hears the parents' implicit messages and starts
to respond to them by acting out in a problematic manner,
the parents can treat the child as if he or she really were

a problem. Thus, a vicious cycle is set into motion. At what point the parents start to treat the child as troublesome and at what point the child internalizes the problems depend on the messages given and the number of times they are repeated.

Thus, it can safely be said that there is no sudden development of problems in a child. It is a gradual process, occurring over a period of time. By the time a person is seen in therapy, a vicious cycle may already be in place. Unless the child is young, it becomes somewhat more difficult to effect change by removing external forces, because the older child or adult has internalized the role of scapegoat. Frequently, the older, disturbed child adds stability to the family system, and once this has taken place, the scapegoat role cannot be passed easily from one to another.

In families who have moderate rather than severe problems, the scapegoating process may shift from one child to another. Usually repetitive patterns of interaction occur, not due to any one person's sickness or internal conflicts, but such patterns are useful for the viability of the entire family system. Each family member's behavior is influenced by the state of the family system at any given moment, and if a needed role is not played by one member, it must be played by another (Sieburg, 1985).

THE RATIONALIZATION OF SCAPEGOATING

In a study by Vogel and Bell (1981), parents expressed considerable guilt about the scapegoated child. When children were identified by neighbors, teachers, and others as being deviant in their behavior, the parents felt guilty and this outside pressure forced them to seek help. Parents did not have much difficulty in explaining why they were concerned about the child, too. However the parents rationalized their own conflicting, inconsistent messages or aggressive behavior toward their children.

Parents' Perception as Victims

In the therapy sessions, some parents saw themselves as "victims" of the poor behavior of the problem child. They spent a lot of time discussing how they coped with the problems that the child had created for them. These rationalizations appeared to remove some of the parents' guilt for victimizing their child. The children's behavior served as a continuous justification for the annoyances expressed toward their child.

Other parents emphasized how lucky the child was to have been born into their family. They were giving the child more than he or she could ever have hoped to get anywhere else. This rationalization would be used to take things away from children, including toys, privileges, and other items that they wanted. The parents also refused to recognize their children's pleas that they were not getting what they really needed. These parents saw themselves as martyrs who lived without any privileges, contending that nothing was ever done for them when they were young but they are doing their best for their own children. Most parents mentioned the fact that their children have more things and also enjoy more freedom than children of an earlier generation—for example, themselves. Many of the parents who punished their children harshly also mentioned that their own parents were much stricter.

Many of these parents gave their children implicit signals to break the rules, but when they were confronted with this fact, they denied doing so. The parents saw the scapegoated child's behavior as willful, bad behavior. Most of these parents felt that the problem child needed to be reprimanded and sternly punished. Neither the advice nor the help of outsiders such as a teacher or counselor was seen as useful because they considered their children's character negative; they denied that they were scapegoating a specific child. One of the myths commonly heard was, "We treat all our children alike." Only rarely did the parents acknowledge that they treated the scapegoated child differently. Their rationale was that they had treated all the children alike, and if a particular child was not behaving well, that child had to be treated differently; and the only way to deal with such a child was through physical punishment and denial of privileges.

Overaffection Toward Opposite-Sex Child

Another form of parental behavior is depicted in the following manner: Some mothers develop an overly strong affection for a son, and some fathers do likewise with a daughter. The strong affection turns to anger and the indulgence to distressful punishment if that child disobeys the parent. In some sense, the general interaction that the parent has with this particular child satisfies the need of the parent for the spouse, who is often not available; the parent thus develops a love-hate relationship with the child of the opposite sex. Although this behavior has a highly defensive quality about it, the parents act as if their behavior were in touch with norms of the outside world. However, in cases of serious distortions in reference to children, parents will come to therapy with unrealistic ideas about how external social norms should apply to them.

> For example, 10-year-old Keith was his mother Carrie's favorite child. Keith spent a great deal of time with his mother, who gave him all her attention. The father was rarely available, either emotionally or physically, and he held two jobs— a clerk and a cab driver. Often Carrie would brag that Keith could do no wrong.
>
> However, one day when Keith returned home an hour late from school due to an extracurricular activity, Carrie locked him out of the house. She refused to listen to any explanations or his pleas that he had informed her earlier about this activity. It was a cold, rainy evening so Keith started to cry loudly. The neighbors who witnessed the mother's behavior called the police.
>
> In therapy Carrie criticized her neighbors and the police for not being understanding to a good, caring parent like herself and for letting Keith "get away" with his behavior.

With families who are not so disturbed, there is an attempt to express emotions to children in a more acceptable manner. In any event, in the dysfunctional families it is necessary to keep the family in balance—a state that requires the coordination of many subtle and inconsistent feelings and behaviors. This behavior is in effect an "armed truce," and the danger of explosion is very real (Vogel & Bell, 1981).

FUNCTIONS AND DYSFUNCTIONS OF SCAPEGOATING

Functions

One of the functions of scapegoating is that it can serve as a personality- and a system-stabilizing force. When parents have severe personal or marital conflicts, the projection of these conflicts onto their children helps to maintain the self-esteem needed to preserve the marriage. One of the important functions of the family is to maintain its solidarity as a source of identification and security for its members. However, in many disturbed families a number of forces appear to threaten that solidarity. Normally couples who scapegoat one of their children are able to encapsulate problems and anxieties that might otherwise destroy the family. Moreover, there is added solidarity between such parents who stand united against the "problem child." The fact that a child is disturbed permits parents to perform the tasks that are necessary to maintain the household and family without having to look at themselves.

Dysfunctions

In families with chronic illness, scapegoating can be viewed as coping behavior to deal with issues that do not disappear. This is also true of the affectively disturbed family, the alcoholic family, and the violent family.

Another problem occurs when the scapegoated child retaliates against his or her parents' ill-treatment through fighting, stealing, drinking, or truancy—thus punishing the parents for their poor treatment. Many children become very skilled in arousing their parents' anxiety and may consciously bungle a task that their parents want them to do. Oftentimes it is the mother who faces counteraggression from the child. In many cases it is the mother who seeks treatment first. She may tolerate a certain degree of hostility from the child, but if the child gets out of control, the mother may be willing to go to great measures to work on the child's problems (Vogel & Bell, 1981).

Sometimes behavior that was tolerated and even encouraged at home is not acceptable in the school setting. School becomes a crucial problem for most of these parents and children. Either the parents are angry with their own children for the problems that occur in the school, or they are angry with the teachers for all the problems that are present in the school setting. If the child is recognized as having a special problem at school, this development appears to make matters difficult for the parents, who may have hoped that the problems would be glossed over (Vogel & Bell, 1981).

The reactions of neighbors, friends, and relatives are added incentives for the family to work on their problems. But what this really means is that the relatives and neighbors are critical of the family of the severely scapegoated child, and therefore the family makes the greatest effort to get rid of the child's maladaptive behavior. Their efforts may take the form of punishing and rewarding the child's behavior.

When the child's behavior gets negative attention outside the family, some husbands and wives blame each other for all the problems. A mother may feel that her husband should spend more time with the child, and the father, in turn, may feel that the child should be better taken care of by his wife. Thus, blaming reappears in the family, and if the marital problems escalate, the child as a scapegoat would be forgotten. However, in most cases, the aggression is directed predominantly toward the child rather than toward the spouse.

The child's personality is affected most by these problems. The child has played the assigned role for a long time and as a result has experienced sufficient personality impairment. The development of emotional disturbance is simply a part of the process of internalizing the conflicting demands placed on him or her. Temporarily, a child gets rewarded for playing such roles, but in the long run, the cost is very high. While it might be said that the scapegoating function is useful to some families as a group, it is dysfunctional for the family, for the emotional health of the child, as well as for his or her adjustment to the outside world.

In the following chapter, the multifaceted aspects of scapegoating will be presented. This will include what it feels like to be a scapegoat and the behavior and history of scapegoaters. The patterns and long-term effects of scapegoating will also be discussed.

2

Inside the Scapegoat,
the Scapegoater,
and the Family

A FAMILY SCENE

Alice waited impatiently for her husband. Harry
had promised to return home at 6:00 P.M., and
now it was past eight o'clock. She was ready. She
wore his favorite lilac-colored, low-necked dress
and his favorite perfume, but Harry did not
come. Why was he late? Why had he promised if
he could not keep his word? "He promised, he
promised," she muttered. Why did he not call?
At least he could explain.

The television was loud. Donald, their oldest
son, was talking at the top of his voice and
imitating a fight on TV. Alice muttered to herself,
"God, can't he stop it! It's nerve-wracking. He's
such a pain!"

Alice shouted, "Donald, lower the volume,
there is too much noise here."

"Okay Mom."

Alice paced restlessly. Eight-thirty P.M. and still no Harry! The television was still too loud. Alice ran to the living room and shouted, "Donald, stop it, I can't stand it!" and shut off the TV. Donald turned it back on. Alice screamed, "Donald, shut off the TV or I will kill you."

The 15-year-old replied, "You're angry because Dad hasn't come home on time, so don't yell at me. I didn't do anything."

Nothing mattered. Alice was furious. She screamed again and threw a vase at Donald. He ducked; the vase hit the window and cracked the glass. "Donald, you are terrible, you are terrible," she screamed. Donald fled from the house. The four other children watched Alice in silence. She ran to the bedroom, weeping loudly.

Donald did not return until 10:00 P.M. He climbed a tree to get to his second-floor room and crawled through a window to avoid his angry mother.

Harry came home at 11:00 P.M. Alice had changed into her housecoat. Her eyes were red from crying. He had forgotten his promise.

"You are terrible," she screamed at her husband, a loud domineering policeman.

"What did you say?" he bellowed in an authoritative tone. There was no response. "There was an emergency at the station, and I had to fill in for another cop."

Alice, frightened of her husband, sobbed softly.

"What's wrong?" he asked. "Can't you understand that I need to work hard to bring home money? You know I have two jobs—you make it hard on me."

Alice cried, "I know. It's not you. It's Donald— he's terrible and troublesome. He gave me a lot of trouble. See the living room window? He broke it—he's terrible."

Harry said, "I'll take care of him. He's terrible, I know. He's always troublesome. Where is he?"

"He ran out of the house around eight o'clock and hasn't come back."

"What?" Harry roared. "I'll fix him. Let me check his room."

Harry climbed the stairs to Donald's room and looked in. Donald, wide awake and aware of being the "bad kid," closed his eyes and pretended to sleep. His father left the room.

Harry informed his wife, "I'll take care of him tomorrow." Alice then wept to herself. They had a problem on their hands—Donald!

WHAT IT FEELS LIKE TO BE A SCAPEGOAT

Through the preceding case study we met the scapegoat— Donald. The oldest of five children, he had been scape-goated since the age of three. In a scapegoating family, there are different influences on the child and the adults. In scapegoated persons two aspects of the personality develop: the alienated, passive, tormented, fragmented accuser self, and the compensatory role that the child plays, not only as the suffering victim, but also as the savior of the family. Because the child has received subtle per-mission to play the role, his or her energies are not channeled into constructive behavior, but are split and disruptive and, in many serious cases, frightening. Often, in therapy, scapegoated children behave in a bizarre manner. They are angry and tormented by family issues and are vulnerable to feeling responsible for the various problems in the family.

> Jack, a 13-year-old boy, walked into my office with one purpose in mind: to upset me and make me angry, too, so that he could tell himself he was still the bad kid in the family as well as outside of it. He walked in flapping his arms as if he had no control over them, made faces, appeared to be angry with me, and was immensely disruptive to the point that I was ready to *join* him and act out his disruptive behavior to show him how it affected others. Yet there was another side of Jack that he showed only when he could not help it. A "little boy lost" look came into his eyes when he received no judgment about his behavior. Jack resembled a puppy wanting to be petted, but he was unsure if that petting would hurt or feel comfortable. All Jack had experienced within his chaotic family was being collectively blamed for everything that went wrong by every family member. What he had never known was the security of love, discipline, and family structure.

"I Feel Guilty, Inferior, Anxious"

What I saw in this child was a mixture of desire to accept me and an uneasiness about the positive relationship that was present. Jack was burdened with guilt, feelings of inferiority, and a high degree of anxiety resulting from the lack of a healthy, rewarding connection to his family. Guilt was present because Jack saw himself as responsible for his parents' rejection. Yet he had an underlying recollection that he was once accepted by his uncle. Perera (1986) indicates that scapegoat-identified persons usually have a faint idea that they were once accepted and tend to feel that there was at least one peripheral person who valued them. This belief sustains the ego and staves off the complete fear and self-hate that leads to more serious problems.

Occasionally, we all feel guilty. However, most scapegoated people feel guilty about almost everything they do, believing anything that goes wrong is their fault. For many people, particularly scapegoated persons, the flowering of guilt is seeded in past threats of punishment or actual punishment that caused them to fear that their parents would withdraw their love. Even if they behaved well, the threats produced guilt. Guilt may cause people to have unfulfilled, warped, or terrorized lives: they punish themselves in ways that lead to grief and sorrow, with the added constant fear of rejection by everyone (Freeman & Strean, 1986).

"I Feel Different From Everybody Else"

How do we deal with people who have been set apart as different? When young children face such alienation, particularly from their parents, they become the carriers of shameful behaviors and attitudes that disrupt relationships and make the parents uncomfortable. The scapegoats' troublesome behaviors are a form of vengeance, because they feel rejected. It is usually the child's relationship with the parents that triggers the child's behavior, which in turn makes the child into the scapegoated rejected person. In severe scapegoating, the parents see the child as frightening and hateful. The child who is sensitive to the parent shows depressed and distressed behavior, but as the child accepts the scapegoated role, the *signs* of distress are replaced with acting-out behaviors. This acting out becomes a *signal* to others to remove the stress by punishments or rewards or an inconsistent combination of the two.

Many parents of scapegoated children have a low or moderate level of self-differentiation. This can be further connected to Bowen's concept of a multigenerational transmission process. Bowen visualizes the development of the dysfunctional person as a consequence of several generations of poor to moderate differentiation, triangulation, and inadequate emotional fulfillment. Changes in degrees of differentiation within families occur rapidly or slowly (Bowen, 1976).

Due to their moderate or low level of self-differentiation, scapegoated individuals may have difficulty distinguishing between various emotional states within themselves, such as anger, hurt, sadness, and joy. Sometimes scapegoats cannot distinguish between what is part of self and what is not in terms of responsibilities, role allocation, perceptions, ideas, and opinions, and they do not know how to assert themselves helpfully and harmlessly in a situation.

When people become ashamed of themselves and are beset with socially unsanctioned urges and feelings, they become alienated from self. When they are ashamed of themselves, they label their feelings and behaviors as bad or despicable.

"I Feel Insecure and Unloved"

One of the principal emotional states that we would like all young people to develop is the feeling of security within a family. Often this security is not gained because of dyfunctions and/or inconsistencies as mentioned in the previous chapter. Also, lack of love in the family leads to feelings of inferiority. One of the most significant factors leading to feelings of insecurity is that children are faced with new situations too many times in their lives. A child may be encouraged or discouraged by the birth of a new sibling, the first day at school, a new teacher, and the first contact with playmates. A child's response to new situations is partially determined by his or her previous experiences. If a child is told in new situations that he or she cannot perform, he or she learns to fail. Later, the child responds to new situations accordingly, that is, with fear and uncertainty.

"I'm the Outsider"

One way of looking inside the scapegoat is to redraw the family boundary so that the scapegoat is outside of it. When the scapegoated person is pushed out of the family psychologically, everybody else in the family is "good" and the scapegoat contains all the badness and "causes all the trouble." As the scapegoated child is viewed as a "bad" person, everyone else has the opportunity to express their bad feelings with the excuse that it is the scapegoat's fault that they have to behave so badly toward him or her. When the stress level is very high in the family, more and more painful feelings get loaded on the scapegoated person.

The scapegoated person accepts this role, for it is far better to be blamed for everything and have the family together, than to face the fear that the parents may not stay together or tear each other to pieces and/or abandon the children or commit suicide. So in a peculiar way, the scapegoat feels needed. The family does need him or her and, in turn, the scapegoated person accepts the role that gives him or her some sense of security (Skynner & Cleese, 1983). The same process happens if the scapegoated child is seen as the "perfect child." This person is viewed as the outsider and has to do everything right all the time, and when the stress level is high, he or she receives signals to make everyone "happy."

Scapegoated individuals experience the sense of being chosen. Scapegoats also see themselves as omnipotent people, omnipotent in the sense of being the sin carrier or the "grace carrier." Many scapegoated children are intelligent and sensitive, but through long experience as the family scapegoat, they become accustomed to taking responsibility for problems they encounter in interpersonal relationships. Such people seem alienated, but they are connected to their families whose problems they take on. They are victims by virtue of being chosen to carry the evil and guilt of others, an experience that makes it hard to separate individual and collective responsibility (Perera, 1986).

"I'm Afraid to Speak Up; I'm Afraid to Act on My Instincts"

Many scapegoated persons fear being assertive. They are taught that it is bad to be assertive and are punished for assertive behavior. They tend to deny their self-assertive instinct and passively accept abuse.

Parents who scapegoat want their children to be perfect, but unfortunately children cannot reach such extraordinarily high standards. Nevertheless, children continue to try, believing that there is only one way to achieve a measure of control and security in a difficult world. A child's need to reach these high goals are powerful parental projections that destroy the scapegoated child's relation to her or his own assertiveness as well as dependency needs. Parental projections are their own internal needs and desires that are transferred to the child. Thus, such scapegoated children tend to be overly sensitive and *shadow* the needs and desires of their parents. Shadow refers to attitudes, behaviors, and emotions that do not conform with the ego ideals or the superego, which reflects goodness and morality. As Jung (1953–1979) explains, shadow is the negative side of personality, that is, the sum of all the unpleasant qualities we like to hide. To the family, the scapegoated child embodies all the negative qualities of the family. The child, in turn, begins to believe that he or she is the embodiment of trouble. Instead of negative aspects of behavior being considered as part of one's humanity along with the positive, the parents of scapegoated children see only the bad (Perera, 1986). This shadowing of parents is threatening, and the child develops personal qualities to cover up and mediate for these projections.

Scapegoated children find themselves in a multiple bind. They cannot reach the lofty goals of the scapegoaters and consequently feel they are worthless as well as endlessly guilty. This represents the undifferentiated family ego mass and emotional stuck-togetherness, described by Bowen in a context of emotionality, which floods the intellect, creating an emotional atmosphere from which the less differentiated adult and the emotionally ruled child is controlled by his or her own emotions and by the prevailing emotional climate of the family. Bowen uses the term "emotional process" to describe the responsiveness by which one family member reacts automatically to the emotional state of another, without either one of them being conscious of what is happening. The degree of involvement that a family member experiences in the family ego mass is dependent on the intensity of the emotional process and on the functional relationship of the individual to the central "mass" at the moment (Bowen, 1972). There is no perceivable differentiation between self and object and, often, a person's identity is suppressed because of the wish to avoid collective conflict (Simon, Stierlin, & Wynne, 1985). Minuchin calls this enmeshment. According to Minuchin and others, enmeshed family members have extreme difficulties in defining their roles and functions and they are unable to structure their relationships. This type of confusion helps them to avoid direct confrontations and clarifications, which could be a threat to family unity (Minuchin et al., 1967).

This kind of enmeshment and negative role responsibility is shown in the form of realistic rage and need by the scapegoated child who is constantly split between rage and guilt. Thirteen-year-old Nathan's parents wanted him to be a medical doctor although he could not even spell simple words or write a sentence. At the same time, he was ridiculed about his poor written English. Nathan always seemed to feel guilty that he could not reach up to his parents' expectations, but he was also filled with rage for the unfair, ridiculing treatment received for his efforts to improve his language.

Scapegoats cannot confront others' feelings or their

own. Nathan's mother complained that Nathan was stupid and also puny enough to be bullied by boys in school whom he could not confront. But the demand was paradoxical. He was scapegoated at home and was considered a weakling. His three younger brothers were allowed to bully and boss over him. If he fought back, he was always punished. Thus, Nathan grew up learning to accept his passive role in the family. How is a person to be assertive outside the home when assertion is discouraged within the family? Bringing such contradictions to the attention of the scapegoated person leads to more helplessness and guilt, which add fuel to the self-hate of the person. This has to be worked through in therapy, when the opportunity arises.

"I'm Angry, Full of Rage"

Occasionally, the pent-up rage of the scapegoated person may erupt in a powerful accusatory outburst, which just "seems to happen" to the individual and leaves a residue of remorse as well as guilt (Perera, 1986). Let's look at 14-year-old Anthony.

> Persistent, precipitating negative episodes with a young boy eventually led Anthony to choke this boy in a residential setting. This incident was prevented from becoming fatal by the cottage parent in the agency who jumped in to help the victim. After half an hour had passed, Anthony was full of remorse and guilt. He did not know what had made him angry; he could not explain himself to others. Anthony promised that he would never do such a thing ever again. However,

such episodes that he precipitated happened habitually.

Often these individuals have a constant ego-maiming need to purify and denature assertiveness until it is expressed only in passive-aggressive modes.

In another situation, 10-year-old Mark would sit in therapy and play with his fingers. He would talk endlessly about his "green" thumb as well as his pets, which varied from a rat to a spider. Sometimes he would come late for a therapy session and seem preoccupied. Mark did little things to annoy me, in spite of a congenial relationship. If we talked about something, he might pretend that he did not hear me or he would ask me to repeat it to him a number of times. His grudging responses were often rude one-word answers. When I expressed annoyance, he would respond in a sarcastic monotone. "I am really sorry," which was meant to further provoke me.

I saw his passive-aggressive behavior as an expression of his deeply felt anger and as an example of the way he set himself up to be scapegoated.

THE SCAPEGOATING RELATIONSHIP

Scapegoaters: How Do They Feel?

Who are the parents of these children? Let us call them scapegoaters. How do they feel about scapegoating their children? Do they enjoy it? Are they the "bad guys"? As discussed previously, the scapegoater's behavior is an attempt to keep the family together. How does the scapegoater feel when faced with the responsibility of dealing with a scapegoated child?

> Eric's parents had scapegoated him, the oldest child, for many years. When his behavior became unmanageable at home and at school, they placed him in a residential treatment center. When the boy's therapist said that he was ready to return home, Louise, Eric's mother exclaimed that she was afraid. She feared his behavior and his temper tantrums. Was she not a part of his growth and development? In fact, was she not part of his life and also part of his problems? In therapy sessions, Louise cried a number of times, expressing her fears that he would not get better and she would not know how to handle him.

Louise's behavior is fairly common among scapegoaters. They have a profound fear of confronting their own helplessness and usually defend their helplessness by concrete actions and attempts to find a practical solution to every problem. They also tend to read emotional messages as being concrete and, thus, misinterpret the child's affect as a physical fact, a concrete demand, or a globalized statement (Perera, 1986).

> When 10-year-old Julie yelled in exasperation "I hate you" at her younger brother, Gordon had been teasing and taunting her for over an hour. Their mother, Hilda, punished Julie severely.

The mother literally assumed that Julie "hated her brother" Gordon and viewed it as a global statement.

Lacking any understanding of the process, the scapegoated child exacerbates the scapegoater's feelings of helplessness by his or her sudden bursts of anger and acting-out behaviors. Many scapegoaters, who have rigid and brittle egos, cannot tolerate this behavior, and their responses in turn lead to escalating patterns of rejection that the child is forced to experience. Subtly the child is aware that the parents are fearful of confronting emotional as well as symbolic reality, but the scapegoat is overpowered by the role of the victim.

Often Louise talked concretely: "We gave Eric so much. Why can't he shape up?" At one point, she mentioned, "He should be better than us," referring to herself and her husband. To my further questioning, Louise responded, "We did not have food on the table three times a day when we were growing up; we did not have such fine clothes. He has a color TV and a room to himself, which is always untidy. He has all the opportunities for a good education and he won't use it." How do you tell these apparently well-meaning parents that the problem is not solely concrete and physical? These parents, who have brittle egos, have denied dormant impulses that come to the forefront in the security of the home atmosphere. It was in this home setting that Eric was physically and emotionally abused by his parents.

Their reasoning was always simplistic: "I was angry and threw things, and they fell on Eric." Once Louise threw a hot cup of coffee on Eric. It burnt the side of his face but did not leave any physical scars. She sighed and said, "No damage done." Again, the emphasis was on the physical.

At times, scapegoaters observe their own personalities projected in their children, and being fragile people themselves, they attack the scapegoated child. Diane once mentioned that she could not stand to see her daughter get angry. The daughter's face would become knotted and she would turn an ugly blue. Diane was describing herself as well. However, she remained unaware that this description fit her as well.

The Family History of Scapegoaters

What is the family history of scapegoaters? Many of them are victims, too. They do not have strong egos, and they are likely to be the weak and hurt children of overdemanding and self-righteous parents. Usually these adults also suffer from guilt that is partially repressed. Quite often, there is strong bonding between the scapegoated child and the scapegoater.

Sixteen-year-old Pam came home every afternoon as soon as school was over to care for her disabled mother. She did not participate in any school extracurricular activities, though all she faced at home was pain and ridicule. It is true that the mother needed the daughter's care, but the child had unmet needs as well.

The child being available to the scapegoater is partially projection and partially an assessment that the child makes in terms of understanding the unmet parental needs. A love-hate relationship is often seen among adult children and their parents.

> Another classic case is that of 40-year-old Stella, whose 65-year-old mother, Leslie, lived in Stella's house as her dependent along with Stella's grown-up, unmarried sisters. Stella had been involved in a car accident in which her father and her brothers were killed instantly. Stella felt guilty that she survived. Leslie made it worse and blamed Stella for the car accident, saying that if Stella had not been crying, her father may not have wanted to take her out for a ride! This incident happened when Stella was 10 years of age. But her mother continued to hold her responsible 30 years after the father's death.
> Stella developed a strong feeling of guilt and believed that she was responsible for her father's and her brothers' deaths, though it was clear that the father had other business to take care of that evening. A strong love-hate bond developed between Stella and her mother. At times she cried, "I want to hit my mother, but I can't. She is a phony and a bitch just like I am." Stella was afraid of her mother's sharp tongue because Leslie would retaliate quickly, but at the same time Stella was aware of her mother's dependency.

Sometimes the scapegoated child verbalizes the nascent awareness of the splits or the projective identification. Both Stella and her mother suffered from them, albeit in different ways. As a defense mechanism, in splitting, the conscious identity is fragmented and split because there is denial or automatic evasion of the experience by the ego. For instance, a victim of incest does not remember the sexual acts with an adult family member because the victims believe that their minds left their bodies at the door of the room where the incest took place, thus splitting the body and the mind. As one client recalled, "It was not me, because my mind was not there." Grotstein (1985) describes projective identification as a mental mechanism whereby the self experiences the unconscious fantasy of translocating itself or aspects of itself that is either good, bad, negative, or positive into another person or object for defensive purposes. These concepts will be presented in greater detail while dealing with the healing process in the next two chapters.

The gravely scapegoated person is habitually made to feel responsible for many of the unacceptable events that happen in the family and, hence, a guilty conscience becomes a way of life. The scapegoat observes the unacceptable shadow qualities of the scapegoaters and feels responsible for them. Such a person is hypersensitive to ethical and emotional issues and easily accepts the roles of caretaker and nurturer.

THE FAMILY CONTEXT: WHO IS THE VICTIM?

Who is the victim in intergenerational scapegoating? It is difficult to blame anyone or view one as a victim and another as a scapegoater.

> In a difficult case, two sons, Wilbur and Vincent, aged 14 and 15, were alternately sexually abused by their mother, Miriam. They were placed in a

residential setting and saw one another as rivals for the mother's love; they consequently hated each other. One time they tried to hurt each other physically when the mother was overtly affectionate to one son in front of the other. In therapy the mother was very talkative as well as very infantile. She talked about herself, her sons, and her father, who had sexually abused her. She was afraid to have both sons together with her in therapy. She mentioned that it was almost like having too many grown-ups in one room and she could not handle it.

As the chosen one by her father, Miriam was justifying her behavior to me. So how was I to deal with the scapegoated child, Wilbur, her chosen victim, who according to Miriam was not as well behaved as his older brother?

Therapy with Miriam started with her boyfriend in attendance. He accompanied her out of fear that she would get lost on her way to the agency. Since the agency was located 20 miles from her home and she was "good on roads," I found his attitude a little overprotective. While in session Miriam mentioned, with her boyfriend by her side, that she was doing her sons a favor, just as her father had done for her. She had been sexually abused—her term, "introduced to sex"—by her father, who had promised to teach her everything. In addition, Miriam's father's sisters (her aunts) had also been sexually abused by their father (her grandfather). Therefore, she questioned what was wrong about introducing her sons to sex.

There had been a chronic transactional pattern in this family, one that had apparently existed for a long time, and through it, dysfunctional structures had arisen. How was I to deal with this family to help them function realistically when their reality had been distorted for two generations or more? What happened in Miriam's life was painful, for she was still the burden bearer for her family. Her father died suddenly in his early forties. Miriam married in a hurry, to the "wrong man" as she called him, who lived in her home with her siblings and her mother. After four years of misery, they divorced and he moved away. Miriam was left with two sons, her mother, and a number of her siblings, for whom she had to provide. Miriam's mother herself was apparently the silent witness or the ghost in the family until her husband died. After her husband's death, the mother accused Miriam of taking her husband away. Apparently the father did not sexually abuse his other daughters. Miriam was guilt-ridden by the constant accusations of her mother and felt an intense obligation to take care of her family.

Boundary Problems

As Miriam unraveled her life history, chronic boundary problems among family members emerged. Boundaries, as described by Minuchin (1974), define who participates and how they participate in family interactions. Minuchin says that the function of the boundary is to protect the differentiation of the system. Every family system has specific functions and demands made on its members, and the development of interpersonal skills achieved in these subsystems is predicated on the subsystem's freedom from interference from other subsystems. Ordinarily, in an effectively functioning family, all types of negotiations are possible because the family system is governed by clear and flexible boundaries, but Miriam's family was dysfunctional. In dysfunctional families, typically all subsystems use the same member to diffuse subsystem conflicts. Miriam was used to detour or deflect the large number of spousal conflicts her parents had to deal with constantly. However, as Minuchin demonstrates, a rigid triad developed between Miriam and her father (and the mother as the outsider) that ended in a sexual relationship.

Here, the boundary between the parental subsystem and the child became diffused and the boundary between the parents-child triad became inappropriately rigid (Minuchin, 1974). Thus, Miriam and her father were rigidly bound in a cross-generational coalition against the mother.

How do cross-generational coalitions come into being? If problems are poorly resolved, one parent may unite with a child in a coalition against the spouse, which results in keeping the spouse peripheral (Minuchin & Fishman, 1981). However, in Miriam's life, this coalition came to an abrupt end when the father died. Miriam mentioned repeatedly that her parents did not get along with each other. If the father wanted anything urgently, be it food or a shirt that needed to be ironed, her mother did not mind letting Miriam do her work. When her father died, Miriam felt paralyzed with pain because her mother constantly and bitterly attacked the dead father as well as Miriam. Miriam was angry because she had loved her father, but she was not sure whether she should defy her mother or listen to her. She was overwhelmed with guilt and felt obligated to listen to her mother. The mother had subtle power to effect or resist changes in the family. Thus, in many ways the dysfunctional transactional patterns in the family were maintained and carried over to the next generation.

The Scapegoating Environment

Miriam was the family's scapegoat and played her role well. What are the rules that these scapegoated children live by? They develop what is called the scapegoat complex. Scapegoated children have a tremendous capacity to bear pain because they view themselves as deserving it and have experienced it sufficiently to want to own it. Scapegoats are people who have been overstimulated while young to satisfy parental needs, either psychological or physical, or else they tend to be uncommonly sensitive by nature. Such children are perceived by their parents as understanding and knowing more than they should. This characteristic frightens the scapegoating parents who, in turn attempt to disregard or deny the child's perceptions through shaming or rejecting them. Because parents are powerful, the child, as in Miriam's case, develops a confused relationship with the parent. Though Miriam loved her father because he was the only one who was really good to her, she was also confused because deep down she knew that what her beloved parent did was wrong. Such children do not notice the harm that is done to them because they lack sufficient objectivity. They approach intolerable situations with an innocence and a naivete that is difficult to imagine. Often these children return to the abuser hoping to discover the good parent who might be redeemed. But this seldom happens. As Miriam said, "This was my father. He was always kind and caring toward me. No one told me it was awful when he abused me. I personally thought it must be okay, since my father knew so much, . . . except my mother was angry."

According to the scapegoating from which a person suffers, he or she can perceive reality only through a distorting rigidity that could be equated with conscientiousness and judgmentalism. Habitually scapegoated people's self-images are negative. Scapegoats feel guilty and miserable and identify themselves as falling short and as being bad and wrong (Perera, 1986). Yet scapegoats may view the scapegoaters as saviors. They can be understanding to the point of absurdity and they are willing to forgive in others shortcomings they would truly condemn and despise in themselves. Many of these people suffer from self-hate because it is difficult for them to jump back and forth through the perceptual splits of seeing the good and the bad without being torn by the inconsistencies of the double standards they have created for themselves, which keeps them "in a double bind."

The Double Bind

The ingredients of a double bind could be described as follows: Two or more persons involved in an intense relationship that has a high degree of physical and/or psychological survival value for one, two, or all of the concerned. Situations in which intense relationships exist include family relationships and relationships involving material dependency, friendship, love, and a cause or ideology. Contents of this relationship are influenced by social norms, tradition, and feelings.

In such situations, a message is given which asserts something; the message also asserts something about its own assertion, and these assertions are mutually exclusive. So, if the message is an injunction, it must be disobeyed to be obeyed; if it is a definition of the self or of the other, the person thereby defined is this kind of person only if he or she is not, is not if he or she is. The meaning of the message is therefore undecidable (Watzlawick, Beavin, & Jackson, 1967).

Thus in a double bind there is a primary negative injunction and a secondary injunction conflicting with the first, and like the first, the second injunction is enforced by punishments or signals that threaten survival; and last there is a tertiary negative injunction prohibiting the victim from escaping the field (Okun & Rappaport, 1980).

A NO-WIN SITUATION

> A family consists of a young girl, Jennifer, and her mother and father. The girl is constantly given the message that she does not "show enough consideration" for her parents. When Jennifer "approaches" her parents to show consideration, she is told, "You are crowding us; don't interrupt or intrude in our privacy." When she retreats to show consideration for their privacy, she is told, "You do not care about us, stop ignoring us!" Jennifer is 11 years old and is trapped in a *no-win* situation.

TRANSGENERATIONAL SCAPEGOATING

At the transgenerational level in scapegoating families there is an inability to contribute to the next generation's survival and well-being, and this breaks the family down in every psychological sense. Parents do not earn their entitlement in the language of Boszormenyi-Nagy and Krasner (1986), because they do not offer responsible care to the young. Entitlement is an ethical "guarantee" that arises within a relationship and accumulates merit on the side of the deserving contributor. Briefly, constructive entitlement is the result of *continuing to care* about earning entitlement, and destructive (or vindictive) entitlement is the result of *refusing to care* about earning entitlement— two opposing clinical consequences. The dimension of merited trust or earned entitlement exists in diametric opposition to the dimension of power-based expediency, successful exploitation, social superiority, and winning against a weaker competitor, among other characteristics.

In fact, in scapegoating families there is one-sided exploitation, as in the case of the scapegoated person. Looking from a purely linear, material basis, the more one person can extract from another person, the better off he or she is. In contrast, the benefits that are derived from earned merit are based on what one receives through the process of giving and caring (Boszormenyi-Nagy & Krasner, 1986). These concepts will be discussed further in Chapter 3. Boszormenyi-Nagy and Krasner put it beautifully when they emphasize that a chronically unpaid and cumulative debt is in itself damaging to the perpetrator as well as to the object. In other words, debt damages both creditor and debtor alike.

In intergenerational scapegoating, there are no winners. The scapegoater's future freedom is undermined as he or she becomes tied to the victim. For the child who has been scapegoated from an early age, the process of development of basic trust is undermined. When basic trust is affected, all the person's relationship orientations are affected. Thus, the effects of this one-sided relationship are open ended, unpredictable, and tend to have implications for several generations, unless timely help is offered.

Long-term Effects

In intergenerational scapegoating, pathological trans-actional patterns are created. The destructive aspects of scapegoating in intergenerational situations begin when a child's ability to be destructive appear in direct proportion and relation to the degree to which the adults critically undermine his or her trust. When family members can be helped to convert their concern for each other into action, they can enter into the process of redistributing the burdens and benefits among themselves. This process of redistribution, where each family member takes personal responsibility for his or her own part and terms, can lead to new, more liberating balances of relational justices among family members. It can be further noted that an impeccably just or fair distribution of advantages and burdens is an idealized goal. When parents set up *idealized* adult standards for a child and expect him or her to carry them out, this amounts to a direct road toward their parentification and to their subsequent scapegoating as failures (Boszormenyi-Nagy & Krasner, 1986).

In destructive parentification there is use of projective identification and infantilization of the child by a parent or parents. In families with parentified children, one may assume that the parents' needs have not been met by their own parents, and desire for fulfillment of these needs are transferred to their own children. Thus parentification is seen as a form of delegation, that is, in many ways the children take the role of the grandparents (Simon, Stierlin, & Wynne, 1985). Whatever the intentions of the parents are, destructive parentification leads to possessive dependency of the parents upon the child. This possessive dependency of the parent creates an asymmetrical relationship, placing the child in a captive role. The more this child is made to feel like a helpless captive, the more anger the child accumulates. This gets the child to the point of being overly responsible to the parent(s) and, at same time, punishing and fighting the parent(s) because of his or her position in the family (Boszormenyi-Nagy & Krasner, 1986). As demonstrated earlier in the book, this is a common occurrence in dysfunctional families, which is typically focused on one designated child.

Miriam appears to be such a case. Her relationship with Mother is one of love and hate, with more overt hate than love. Yet she does not choose to leave or remedy the situation as she is caught in the position of not being able to live with Mother and not being able to live without her. Miriam also feels overly responsible for her mother's well-being. Her relationship orientation toward her sons was negatively affected. This intergenerational pathology appears to be long lasting, self-perpetuating, and self-sustaining. Miriam, in her turn, is in a better position to affect her children than vice versa. When her children grow up, they will be in a better position to affect their children than vice versa. In this sense, each intergenerational act is asymmetrical because the filial generation is exposed to different influences as they go through the phases of formative development. People who have been exposed to a lifestyle of scapegoating become defensive, provocative, ambivalent, and suspicious.

Patterns Among the Scapegoated

Scapegoating behaviors are also the result of a series of communications and interactions that create a transactional pattern as well as a structure. In scapegoating, family members can benefit from casting each other in roles that represent internally needed and programmed partners. These rigidly held relational patterns create a unique reference point for each family member's self (Boszormenyi-Nagy & Krasner, 1986).

Often, in family situations when young people are constantly made to feel left out ("the odd one out"), they typically turn their agony inward and perceive themselves as lesser people. Because their personalities are also distorted by the perceptions of the scapegoaters and others, scapegoats begin to think that people dislike them because of the way they look. One 28-year-old woman fretted, "I know I shouldn't ask you this, but do you think I am ugly? My mother was beautiful and she always called me ugly. She looked like Marilyn Monroe. Do you think I am ugly? Maybe if I had her complexion, if my nose was shorter, if I was a little bit shapely, then I would feel all right about myself." Intergenerationally, too, there is a preoccupation with looks. Several generations of scapegoats often have a negative perception of their bodies and of their looks.

Scapegoated persons often seize upon a particular attribute of their bodies and dwell on it as the cause for their sense of alienation. One scapegoated woman remarked, "If only I could talk loudly and clearly, I am sure everyone would like me. But hear my voice. Isn't it terrible? I hate it. This is the reason I cannot make friends." The physical flaw that the person imagines having becomes the physical counterpart for the emotional-psychological state, the cause for shame, and the reason to avoid interactions. As Perera (1986) indicates, the supposed flaw becomes the scapegoat on the bodily level; it cannot be thrust away, for it is the omnipotent physical concomitant of the complex, the rationalization that underlies the self-hatred that is a person's felt identity. In other words the scapegoat finds a scapegoat in his or her own person—a physical flaw that he or she can blame, just as others blame him or her. Usually scapegoats have learned to endure a great deal of pain from a young age. They experience tremendous psychological pain and feelings of rejection and inferiority. Without therapy, they are likely to recreate their own experience in one or more of their offspring.

Multiple Scapegoating

A marriage of individuals with low self-differentiation and/or intergenerational scapegoating legacies could lead to constant turmoil and/or scapegoating of a child. Sixteen-year-old David's case comes to mind.

> David had been the family scapegoat from the time he was eight years old, when his 15-year-old stepsister, Kathleen, ran away from home. Perhaps Kathleen had been the scapegoated child in the family before David. But after she left, nothing that David did was right; his mother would find fault with the way he ate his food and with the way he did his chores at home. Until then, David had done well in his school work, but he suddenly gave up and started to fail in all subjects.
>
> At 16, he was brought in for therapy because he was not coping well at school or at home. I was amazed at the degree of discomfort he bore. David had experienced beatings and ridicule. According to his parents, nothing he did was

right. If it was not his mother, it was his father who was yelling and screaming and punching him.

With a combination of family and individual therapy, David appeared to understand his situation. After a period of rage and blame, when he recognized his problems as the result of his parents' conflicts, David began to consolidate his ego strengths. Unfortunately, the process necessitated an essential estrangement from the scapegoaters, and he achieved a new and realistic acceptance of the rejecting parents. David saw his parents as victims caught in a family cycle from which they could not escape. He found a graceful way out of the scapegoat role when a teacher took an interest in him in high school. David learned to respect this teacher and became more and more academically involved. His teacher, who appeared to be a positive role model, seemed to have a stabilizing effect on him. David spent more and more time with the teacher and eventually got a part-time job. He even complied with his parents' wishes and paid rent for the attic in which he lived. David spent a large amount of time pursuing his academic interests and did not appear to be a problem at home.

At last, David's family seemed to be getting their lives together. But the effects were short lived. One month after David's matters were settled, Betty, David's younger sister, began acting out, getting poor grades in school, playing truant, and taking drugs. It was almost as if she had received a silent message from the family. At that moment, the family regained its former homeostasis. Once again, volatile fighting, heated discussions, and painful teasing took place. If Betty were to get her act together with outside help such as a school teacher and if she had not been too damaged to function on her own, the next child would likely become the designated scapegoat.

Unresolved Problems

Why does multiple scapegoating take place in families? Often, couples who marry may have unresolved issues and problems in their families of origin. They appear to have been arrested in their development. Development involves new challenges, new contexts, and inevitable periods of disequilibrium. However, in families in which scapegoating is an established pattern, the family accepts suffering as their way of life. The family has a tremendous capacity to endure discomfort. Often the spousal system in such families has developed dysfunctional transactional patterns for handling stress. The parents are unable or afraid to confront each other with their issues and problems. Often, a child becomes the designated scapegoat. This normally includes a cross-generational pattern involving the parents and one child. With therapeutic help the family redraws the boundaries, so that the spousal boundaries are strengthened without involving a third person.

In David's family the parental-spousal system appeared to have stopped functioning a long time ago. It was as if the family system could not function without involving another family person. Thus the vulnerable person is hooked into the role of a scapegoated person. In therapy, insightfully, Betty mentioned that even as a child she had felt responsible for the problems of the family. If her brother was not present, all the misbehaviors of the other siblings would fall upon her. At times, when she got angry for being unfairly accused, she was told that her reaction was the proof of her guilt. Even as she grew older, Betty felt that if her brother was not there to take the blame for problems in the family, then they would be her problems. As she matured, Betty continued to equate psychological pain with feelings of rejection and inferiority.

Thus, when David ceased being the scapegoat, the parents turned to the next available person, Betty. Betty felt that her parents had critized her once too often. She was tired of the negative treatment and started to take drugs which, in turn, affected her ability to go to school and to function effectively. As time passed, Betty started to feel guilty for becoming the "troublesome one" but did not see the parental behavior as abuse.

It is only when scapegoated children recognize and view punishments, rejection, and the pain of blame as real abuse that they can work on changing their lives. However, Betty was not ready to deal with the issue of real abuse or the fact that her parents were inadequate people who could not function without tensions in the family. Although the parents had worked with David and the therapist, it appeared that they could not function on their own without using a third person as a scapegoat, and thus a similar scenerio was created between Betty and her parents. The scapegoated person usually finds himself or herself caught in a welter of primitive feelings, punitive as well as pitying, and is confronted with morbid reflections on the unfairness of fate which leaves one person totally helpless.

Family Equilibrium

In multiple scapegoating the functional role played by the scapegoat is the maintenance of family equilibrium by drawing all the problems into himself or herself. In a highly disrupted family, each child experiences a certain degree of conflict as well as rejection. Thus, when one scapegoated child leaves the scene, the family is amply supplied with other children who could be scapegoated to maintain the family homeostasis. In such families the youngest child may not receive permission to leave, which creates the condition for a stalemate that is responsible for keeping the unhappy couple together. Sometimes, such children become arrested in their development and also develop tremendous capacity to endure discomfort.

Many individuals who were scapegoated in their own families are also socialized into the same role when they enter new situations; they are willing to take on the scapegoated role. For example, when two people are attracted to each other, the attraction could be unconscious/subconscious due to their similarity. They could be from two different abused homes. They meet and fall in love, as they see in the other person a "divinely damaged person" like themselves. Thus begins another generation of scapegoating if the couple does not work through their own issues and problems.

The following chapter will deal with the ego structure of a scapegoated person. Issues discussed will include distortions of perception, containing and enduring painful experiences, and problems of assertion.

3

The Personality of the Scapegoated Person

THE EGO STRUCTURE OF THE SCAPEGOATED PERSON

For those who are most scapegoated, the hurt starts at a young age due to the withholding of affection and emotional and, at times, physical nourishment. Such withholding leads to a feeling of deprivation and a sense of being unworthy to receive anything that is valuable. These feelings are derived from the parents' or caretakers' *inability* to give the child valid emotional and physical caring. In fact, adults who have unconsciously chosen a child as a scapegoat treat him or her differently from their other children. When families come for therapeutic help, this is why they point a finger at one child and explain (oftentimes logically) why he or she alone needs help. If the child suffers from medical problems, this is understandable, but when a child is scapegoated, he or she is viewed as the only troublemaker in the family. This designated child grows up without receiving much approval or affection and is used by the family to protect itself from self-destruction. Such children, in turn, are bound to their parents through a sense of loyalty.

Loyalty

The term "loyalty" drives from the French word "loi," which means law. *Webster's Dictionary* (1989) describes loyalty as faithfulness to something to which a person is bound by a pledge, a duty, or a sense of what is right and/ or appropriate. Boszormenyi-Nagy and Spark (1973) describe loyalty as external expectations coupled with internalized obligations. Loyalty can be further defined as an individual's attitude that encompasses identification with the group, relationships with other members, trust, reliability, responsibility, commitment, faithfulness, and staunch devotion. Being loyal in most families is the expression of an unwritten code of social regulations and sanctions. Loyalty of this kind is seen in some school children who develop phobias in order to stay at home with a parent who is lonely and needs companionship.

Indebtedness

It should be noted that loyalty often reflects the awareness or recognition of indebtedness. Indebtedness involves actions that increase one person's entitlement and another person's obligation, expressed in statements such as "I have to help this person now, for without him, I could not have made it." As specified in Chapter 2, Boszormenyi-Nagy and Krasner (1986) indicate that the concept of *need-complementarity* leads to an equally significant and parallel explanatory note, which they term as *entitlement*.

Earned Entitlement

In earned entitlement an individual wins the right and freedom to accept pleasure and enjoy life by offering a measure of care to people (often children) who have invested their care in him or her. Also, grown children earn entitlement through unrequited giving to the next generation. As one generation gives to another, it is also working toward its own destiny. This in turn leads the family members to accrue personal liberation in addition to what the next generation may be able to repay directly.

Destructive Entitlement

Destructive entitlement as seen in serious scapegoating is one end result of parental failure to honor the inherent entitlement with which each infant is born. If nurturant care is seriously withheld from the young and dependent child, it can be said that he or she is unjustly, and often even exploitatively, injured. Parental failure in terms of neglect, emotional or physical, affects the child's merit (Boszormenyi-Nagy & Krasner, 1986). When an adult has not done anything positive for a child, but rather has hurt or misused him or her, such a persecuted child still feels loyalty toward the adult, but this loyalty is a carryover of destructive entitlement, which in turn this child as an adult passes on to his or her own children. Destructive entitlements include chronic imposition of parental distrust, assigning to the child unreachable goals, and manipulation of a child's sense of entitlement. The degree of destructive entitlement involves the child's dependency and helplessness and the scope and intensity of injuries suffered.

Thirty-year-old Travis stated that he still loved and cared about his mother simply because she was his mother. Although his mother had tied him to a crib until he was a-year-and-a-half old and had continuously neglected and abused him, Travis still felt loyal toward her. "I know she was not nice to me, she did not know any better. . . . She is still my mother." Here is recognition and understanding of the fact that this person owes his life to his parent, irrespective of the abuse and neglect he experienced. However, in his relationships with his own children, he was extremely destructive. He was aware that his children should not be abused, but he did not know how to stop his destructive tendencies: all he could fall back on was his own destructive upbringing.

Guilt

When a scapegoated person is not loyal it makes him or her feel guilty. From an intrapsychic perspective, guilt is often assumed to be both irrational and pathological. Guilt itself could be classified as irrational or as realistic based upon how indebtedness is viewed in the family (Boszormenyi-Nagy & Spark, 1973). D. W. Winnicott (1986) initially recognized that the capacity to feel guilty was a significant developmental accomplishment and saw this in the infant's growing ability to maintain relationships. Realistic guilt is like the pain accompanying a wound: it reveals that something is wrong and may serve as a spur for eventual healing in a person. However, some people suffer from pathological guilt. In this situation a person takes on everyone else's guilt. As Karpel and Strauss (1983) indicate, guilty feelings are frequently linked to the fear of betraying another person or actually doing so, which is the ultimate violation of loyalty.

Parentification

In a healthy family, to the degree a child supplements the parents' resources, this can be an avenue of growth and enrichment. Yet, when parents draw heavily upon children, their own life can get sucked into the captive devotion to becoming a parental figure.

Often, scapegoated children feel tremendous guilt and take all of the problems of the family onto themselves. As discussed in Chapter 2, this sometimes happens because of the parents' misuse of authority, which can be explained by parentification—a misuse that disregards the asymmetrical nature of obligations in a parent-child relationship, that is, children are viewed as equals by parents (Boszormenyi-Nagy & Krasner, 1986).

Destructive Parentification

Destructive parentification (Boszormenyi-Nagy & Krasner, 1986) can be described as the use of the child's filial obligation to reinforce his or her constant and almost captive availability to the parents for their own needs. Parentification can take many forms and may include infantilization of a child, possessiveness, and extreme overprotectiveness, all of which can lead to the crippling development of the child's personality. Such children are usually available to parents on a permanent basis to deal with all of the parents' issues.

Some of the worst examples of destructive parentification are seen in cases of addiction and criminality. A young person's anger turned inward can lead to alcohol and drug abuse. Some young people become abusive to others and participate in crimes that do not pay off; their anger is turned against the outside world and their own families in the form of crimes.

Whenever parents fail to take on their own responsibilities as adults, children become recruited to take on overly heavy, crushing responsibilities. But when a child is given adult responsibilities for an explicit period of time, the situation may be healthy, enhancing emotional growth rather than handicapping or exploiting him or her.

However, destructive parentification happens not when a role shift occurs but when relational aspects of a parent-child situation change. In destructive parentification, the child is not acknowledged for what he or she does. Moreover, there are negative guilt-ridden allegations by the parents when matters do not work out well, and there is manipulation of the child to satisfy the parents' own needs. The more subtle the induction and the imposition of guilt, the more the child feels entrapped in this role of destructive parentification. One of the worst examples that I recall is the following case:

> Ten-year-old child, Blake, was recruited to meet her father's needs. This meant accompanying the father on shopping sprees and all outings as the mother was too ill, tired, or busy to go out with him. Thus, Blake played the role of surrogate wife. On her tenth birthday, when the father bought Blake a bouquet of flowers, her mother flew into a rage, called Blake bad names, and accused the child of stealing her husband away from her. In a fury, she ran to the kitchen, picked

up a pair of scissors, and started to cut the young girl's long blond hair because her husband admired the daughter's beautiful hair—what a birthday gift!

This young girl was definitely a parentified child who did not receive any acknowledgment of her role but was also scapegoated for the role she had to play; thus, she lived her life in a double bind. The girl's destructive parentification grew out of necessity because of the mother's supposed weakness and ill health and the father's need for a companion.

All children are entitled to parenting because of their need for care, nurturing, and guidance. Lack of parenting can result in destructive parentification and the child's own build-up of destructive entitlement (Boszormenyi-Nagy & Krasner, 1986). Children who are brought up in this manner have not learned to self-assert from a very young age and have been punished and made to feel that they do not own themselves—body or mind. Such children are ready to become the burden-bearers.

One such child is a young, unattractive, Black 15-year-old by the name of Ben. According to his mother, Riva, he was the only dark child in the family. Riva sighed and added that her mother felt the same way about her and had always been uncomfortable around her. Beyond this point, Riva's insight disappeared. Ben, the oldest child, was soon followed by other children who were much better looking than he. The mother somehow felt that he was different from the day he was born. Often she would become uneasy when he looked at her, *even* when he was an infant. She felt that he had piercing eyes and could see through her. This made her angry and she would turn his face away from her. But as he grew older the feeling that he was watching her and knew more about her and her behavior than he let on made her develop a vehement anger toward him.

This mother had a weak ego and had experienced destructive parenting. She was caught in the need and incessant war for her own nurturing and learned to hate her son. One day, when he was four years old, she became very angry with him and, in a fit of rage, she pulled out his eye. When I met this very angry child, he was using a glass eye. He became the "bad kid" and set fire to the house and also ran away from home a number of times. He accepted the beatings and severe discipline he received when he returned home as appropriate treatment for being "bad." Thus he developed into a person with a weak ego and poor self-image, just like his mother, who could be manipulated by parents or caretakers and who did the same to others.

In situations where parents set up idealized goals for their scapegoated child, the child is ascribed a superhuman degree of perfection and trustworthiness, and this allows parents or adult caretakers to externalize an internal need for a good parent. Sadly but inevitably this idealized person falls short of perfectionistic expectations and then becomes an alleged traitor and target for well-deserved "blame." Thus, when a parent's support and respect for a child's personality is overshadowed by goals that are essentially possessive and self-serving, destructive parentification sets in. This does not mean that the child becomes "adultlike" in a constructive manner, for with standards too high to reach and the subtle lack of support, the child is the target for negative behavior. Normally, destructive idealization is the first step in destructive parentification (Boszormenyi-Nagy & Krasner, 1986).

> In one case, the family brought their oldest child for therapy because he was "the worst kid on the face of the earth." They complained that Dale did not know how to defend himself against his peers, that he was afraid of the kids on his block, and that he was not masculine enough. But his upbringing showed a family who helplessly dumped all their problems on this child. Whether it was the parents relentless marital conflicts or financial problems, Dale was the target of their anger, pain, and failure. He was never allowed to assert himself in the family as he was the "bad kid," but he was expected, at the same time, to be supportive to his parents and to be adultlike. The parents also had very unrealistic standards for him, such as wanting him to be a high performer and exceed in his studies although he was attending a special school for emotionally disturbed children and was below average in his school performance.

It was almost as if the parents had to set these high standards to satisfy their own needs, but they were certain, at least unconsciously, that the child would not be able to reach them.

The scapegoated person's ego is abandoned and depreciated as he or she cannot escape the exploitative and destructive relationship patterns present in the family and, later, in outside relationships. The scapegoaters experience gratification and some benefits in their relationship with the scapegoated. By scapegoating a child, family members develop a favorable self-definition at the expense of the child. Although the scapegoated child plays a very important role in maintaining the family coherence, this is never acknowledged.

Blame

Blame is an important aspect of scapegoating, and the scapegoated person learns to play the villain and accept the blame. However, it is interesting to note that scapegoaters are also victims of their own drawbacks and upbringing. When a person blames another, he or she is protected from facing the nuances of his or her own accountability. As we all know, it is easier to project our imperfections onto somebody else. Regardless of how old the scapegoated person is, according to Boszormenyi-Nagy and Krasner (1986), scapegoating always suggests implicit parentification. Thus, the scapegoat internalizes and learns to take responsibility for someone else's problems and burdens and becomes the burden-bearer of the family.

An example that comes to mind is the case of a mother with 10 children who were born to different men. She was beleaguered by an untrustworthy world and, therefore, set high standards for her oldest son. She insisted that he be completely open with her so that she could trust him. He was 16 and could not talk to his mother about everything. Of course, this child did not reach her high standards for he could not neutralize her longing to see him as being totally trustworthy in this world. In this manner, one of the standards that a scapegoated person has to live up to is overidealization. The child cannot reach the unrealistically high standards and gets targeted for blame.

In another case, 12-year-old Jeremy was caught between two parents in a split loyalty situation where the parents mistrusted each other. Covertly, each parent expected the child to be trustworthy to him or her alone, but on the outside, distrust filled the family atmosphere. Such children are caught between the two parents' conflicting demands. Scapegoated Jeremy was often reproached for his lack of caring. He was blamed for the parents' problems and held responsible for "fixing the family." At the same time, the child never received credit for any of his positive contributions to the family.

Tragically, destructive parentification also creates parental loss and filial loss: that is, parents forfeit their options for self-validation and do not easily develop their own autonomy (Boszormenyi-Nagy & Krasner, 1986).

Caught in a situation from which there is no easy escape, a scapegoated child develops ego qualities that reflect what he or she has received. The child is plagued with mental hurts, conflicts, and deprivations, and sometimes physical wounds. Constant hurt makes the child feel that he or she is not worthy of love. The feeling of unworthiness that the child carries can come through assimilation and by psychic contagion that reflects the caretaker's inability to give physically or emotionally. When the child is totally controlled by others and in spite of the child expressing aggression or anger, this control can create a deep wound in the area of self-assertion. Being caught in the scapegoat complex affects the ego strengths of a person in terms of perception of consciousness, the ability to endure suffering, the lack of capacity for self-assertion and, finally, the need for self-gratification.

DISTORTIONS OF PERCEPTION

Scapegoated children are usually overstimulated by parental needs or oftentimes they are overly sensitive by nature and may perceive and experience all emotions intensely.

Often the agony and unhappiness of the family is projected onto the child. The child is perceived as a dangerous viewer of family happenings that are best left untouched. As previously discussed, the child is seen as the shadow of the family. Confusion also exists in the child's mind as he or she has a love-hate relationship with his or her parents. Often there is some degree of empathetic bond between the parent and the child. Because of this empathetic bond, the child falls into the pattern that is unconsciously required by the parents. Thus, children may approach dangerous or risky situations in an unaware state or as if they are magically protected (Perera, 1986). As often seen in child abuse cases, the child returns to the parent again and again with the hope that he or she might be redeemed.

> Fifteen-year-old Anne lived in a foster home from the time she was five years old; she had been physically abused by her mother. After Anne was placed in foster care, her mother disappeared from the given address, and the child welfare agency lost touch with her. However, when Anne was 15, the mother suddenly got in touch with the foster family by phone and promised to visit

Anne. This happened about three times, but she never did visit. The foster family was unhappy and angry with Anne's mother, but Anne developed a great desire to go and live with her mother, although Anne felt she did not know her. She told the therapist, again and again, "That's my mother and I came from her, and she has a right to punish me any way she wants because she gave birth to me. I feel that I should live with her, because she told me she needs me, and I do not wish to live with my foster parents . . . although they are nice people."

Anne insisted on being with her mother although time and again she had been neglected, abandoned, and disappointed by her. Anne described her: "She is my mother anyway, even though she has beaten me and not fed me." The natural mother made another erratic phone call, saying that Anne came from her (womb) and so she had a right to take her back. Anne's hopes had been built up with great zeal, but the mother did not keep her word and did not even visit Anne.

Instead of being upset with her mother, Anne put her in an exalted position and saw herself as being the troublesome person whom her mother would not visit.

Rigidity—All Good or All Bad

When a child such as Anne has been placed in a scapegoated position for a long period of time, reality for the child becomes a form of distorting rigidity that sees everything as good or bad but never neutral. Because the child is primarily preoccupied with being accepted by the parent, the child is unable to make balanced evaluations of situations. The vitality that comes through seeing and viewing things differently does not prevail. Therefore, the child cannot view materials objectively and the whole situation is lost to the child as she or he clings to one aspect, attempting hopelessly to be accepted by the rejecting parent. Often such children have negatively focused evaluations of themselves. They feel that they will not improve, for they suffer from radical perceptual self-distortions.

Seventeen-year-old Darcy, who had been rejected thoroughly by his family, saw all the evil in the family as coming from within him. He felt that he could not reach any of the positive goals set out in the world and, therefore, he had to get involved in situations where he did not seem to matter, where success and achievement were not the criteria. This individual saw himself as a computer spitting out information that was always negative. As Perera (1986) aptly indicates in her studies, rejected scapegoated individuals see themselves as negative people, filled with negative information, and nothing they do can redeem them from this situation.

Lack of Validity in Own Perceptions

Those individuals who have been severely scapegoated for a long time have little or no trust in the validity of their own direct perceptions of affect, facts, thoughts, and ideas. Thirteen-year-old Murray, who saw himself as a "bad kid," said, "Everyone tells me that I am bad and stupid. Why shouldn't I not believe them." Although this image was unfair and painful, Murray accepted it as the reality of his life. However, his parents who saw him as "lost" set such tyrannical standards, that he could not reach them. Although such a scapegoated person constantly hears only negatives about himself, at the same time the rejection associated with not reaching the standards persists. Eventually the person is forced into more and more self-rejecting isolation. Thus, he gives more credence to the fluctuating, collective family evaluations of the standards that he needs to reach. Until Murray, through therapy or some other form of corrective experience, is able to put all these ideal standards together and unify them as he sees best for himself, he cannot become one whole individual, aware of both his talents and limitations.

Feelings of Condemnation

Often scapegoated persons feel judged and condemned by the scapegoaters whose standards they are unable to reach. Eventually scapegoats feel miserable and guilty and are identified with falling short of standards and for being bad or wrong. They condemn themselves but do not condemn the scapegoater. The scapegoat has been dominated for so long that it seems a herculean effort even to think in terms of scapegoaters' defects. Scapegoated people usually see and judge the scapegoaters more kindly. As previously mentioned, they constantly seek to redeem them and can understand the behavior of the scapegoater to the point of sentimentality. Scapegoats forgive others for the same shortcomings that they cannot forgive in themselves. This makes it difficult for the ego to function (coalesce) as it is caught between the perceptual splits.

The perceptual splits in one's thinking shows one person as all good and presents another as bad, and the scapegoated person identifies with the "bad" qualities.

Splitting as denoted earlier is a universal phenomenon that happens throughout our lives and is also an activity by which the ego discerns differences within the self and its objects or between itself and objects (Grotstein, 1985). In terms of the perceptual splits, this view also reflects the scapegoat's own sense of self but without the inconsistencies present in the double standard that adults project on to him or her. Often, the double standards presented and utilized by a number of scapegoaters is the root of many problems, like self-hate and confusion, seen in scapegoated people.

Scapegoated people learn to condemn themselves at a very young age. When Tony asked his mother why his father did not return home one night, the mother replied that it was Tony's fault that his father was out drinking. So every time the father got drunk, Tony felt responsible, thinking that his father was drinking because he had done something wrong. One day Tony was beaten badly by his father, and when he cried and asked why he was beaten, he was told he deserved it, that he was the "bad kid" who created all the problems in the family and needed to be set right. Thus, at a very young age, this child identified with being the "bad person" and saw himself as evil. He would walk around with his shoe laces untied and his pants zipper open. Tony saw himself with the self-hate that had been passed on to him from his family.

How would such a person describe abusive parents? Tony described his mother as trying her utmost to correct him by being strict yet, poor thing, she did not succeed because he was incorrigible and always in trouble. Again this young man's perceptions of values were split. He remonstrated that his parents were "patient, good parents," but he overlooked the fact that he was mercilessly beaten and severely punished by them. This scapegoated child, caught in the family complex, serves the wholeness and objective reality by taking on the exclusively rejected parts and negative aspects of the family and endowing the other family members with the positives. Thus, Tony lives in darkness as he continues to attribute the negative aspects of his own life and the family's life to himself.

Polarized Aspects of Self

Often in therapy, these polarized aspects of self can be brought into focus and clients can be helped to understand how they see themselves as carrying all the negative qualities of the family. At first clients are shocked, for they cannot see anything in themselves that is productive or positive. As Mike once told me, "You really mean that my handwriting is beautiful? You really mean *that* or are you kidding?" He was giving me, if you will, a way out of this silly dilemma, which he thought I brought upon myself. When I insisted that his writing was good, he was surprised and rejected the idea. Because he had been condemned and devalued for so long, he could not assimilate anything positive in himself.

Many times, oppressively scapegoated people identify themselves as the guilty, incompetent, and rejected person in the family (Perera, 1986). The loyalty that scapegoats feel in their family role is remarkable. Scapegoated people try to reject the beginning empowerment that is offered by the therapist until they are ready. Learning to accept and develop empowerment takes a long time. Often, scapegoats are caught in an either/or situation until they are ready to see both good and bad in themselves and in other people. The scapegoat polarizes everything, and it takes a very secure relationship with a therapist for the person to become aware of this.

This typical distortion that scapegoated persons have in their minds is carried over to body image as well. Another difficult case that I worked with was George (see Chapter 5), who had his lips burned on a stove. At some point in therapy, George explained that this incident was the cause of all his troubles. This flaw (his lips) was seen simplistically as the cause of all his misery. For a long time he did not wish to have eye contact with me and felt that I would dislike him because of his ugly lips. Rationalization was underlying the self-hatred, which is the individual's felt identity. Of course, George did not blame his mother, who had burned his lips in anger when he was caught in inconsistent disciplining by both his parents. He somehow felt that he deserved this gruesome punishment and functioned accordingly.

Thus, in his own small private life, this child suffered from guilt and justification of guilt of psychological and interpersonal functionings. This perception that he was somehow the bad person affected the ways he judged and accepted himself and others. Since valuation and acceptance depend upon conformity and obedience to standardized communal values, any deviations from them, whether intended and conscious or unintended and unconscious, draw blame, censure, ostracism, or punishment from others (Whitmont, 1986). George had lived all his life with the feeling that he did not measure up and was a deviant, having less power than others. In the beginning of therapy, George believed and accepted this image of himself.

CONTAINING AND ENDURING PAINFUL EXPERIENCES

At a very young age, scapegoated children begin to feel unwanted and unaccepted because they are not shown physical affection and often are not even held in the arms of the parents. Affection demonstrated by physical behaviors such as touching, hugging, and kissing to show that a child is loved is not present with reference to this one particular child. Thus, this child misses out on the all-important protective-containing embrace (Perera, 1986). Children without any support feel left out and exiled from the whole family system. To make matters worse, the child feels that he or she is a specially selected specimen, like the proverbial goat chosen for sacrifice.

Basic Fault

The basic fault or the level of the basic fault is a quality present or, as Balint (1968) puts it, inherent in people. This is unlike the oedipal complex in which the individual faces some degree of conflict or, in fact, is inseparable from conflict. At the oedipal level there is a great degree of conflict, but at the basic fault level the person has not experienced conflict. The individual is very willing to accept blame and fault without any conflict. I have found it rather difficult to "click" with these clients because they have a sense of emptiness or deadness and futility. They lifelessly accept everything that is offered, said, or done to them. They only reveal destructive negative behavior that turns people off and this is compounded by scapegoating.

These clients have learned at a young age to feel that there is a fault within them that should be put right. They view a fault, not a complex, not a conflict, and not a situation. Somewhere in the back of their minds they feel that someone has defaulted or failed them. The anxiety surrounding this area is expressed in a desperate demand that the therapist take care of the client and not fail him or her. In physical sciences it can be said that "fault" means a sudden irregularity in the overall structure, an irregularity that under normal circumstances could be hidden, but if strains and stresses occur, they may lead to a break and profoundly disrupt the overall structure (Balint, 1968).

Balint indicates that the basic fault can be traced to considerable discrepancies in the early formative phases of the individual between his or her biopsychological needs and material and psychological care, attention, and affection available during the early years. This creates a state of deficiency, the causes of which can be congenital; that is, the infant's biopsychological needs may be too exacting, as in the case of cystic kidneys and Friedreich's ataxia, but it could also be environmental, and this is important from the therapists' point of view. Environmentally, the care may be insufficient, haphazard, overanxious, overprotective, harsh, rigid, overstimulating, grossly inconsistent, or merely without understanding or indifferent. That is, there is a lack of "fit" between the child and the people who represent the environment.

Balint describes the processes in this basic fault as embedded in the two-person relationship in which only one of the partners matter. This person's wishes and needs are the only ones that count and must be attended to. The other partner (and this could be a child), although believed to be very powerful, does not really matter insofar as he or she is willing to gratify the first partner's needs and desires or decides to frustrate them. Beyond this, his or her personal interests, needs, and desires do not seem to exist.

Balint views basic fault as the primary object relationship. When distortion of this relationship occurs, it affects all the relationships that the child develops. In order to bring about change in the child's behavior, the therapist needs to help the client develop a primitive relationship in the therapeutic situation that corresponds to the client's own compulsive patterns and maintain it in an undisturbed peace until the patient can discover the possibility of new forms of object relationship and experience and experiment with them.

In order to achieve this state, the client has to regress either to the setting or move toward a particular form of object relationship, which is the cause of the original deficiency state or even some stage before it. For some harshly scapegoated clients, this precondition is important before the client can give up his or her own compulsive patterns and develop new patterns that are less defensive and more flexible. This offers him or her greater possibility to adapt himself or herself to reality under less tension and friction than seen hitherto (Balint, 1968).

While the client is experimenting and growing, it is important that the therapist does not present himself or herself as all-knowing or omnipotent because it is very easy for the client to put the therapist in this position and see him or her as a parent figure. Sometimes, clients may regress and expect the therapist to be all-powerful and help them out of their miseries. The therapist can try to help only through providing an environment, but the efforts to struggle, understand, grow, and change must be left with the client. If the therapist promises or hopes to fulfill or deliver, he or she can create insurmountable difficulties for both of them because of the danger of the client becoming too dependent on the therapist.

One of the important factors the therapist has to create with reference to the development of the client is to provide an environment-client relationship, a "facilitating environment" (Winnicott, 1948/1958). As Spitz (1946) notes, the therapist can become "the mediator of the environment." The facilitating environment can be described as the nutritive qualities of the environment where interactions take place between a person and the environment in order to enhance the adaptive capacities of the person who functions within it. In these given circumstances, the therapist as part of the environment creates a congenial therapeutic atmosphere and acts as mediator to help scapegoated clients cope, adapt, and grow.

Scapegoats see their strengths and reactions to others as the cause of pain. All the pain is viewed as punishment for not being "good." As one client explained, whenever there were problems in her home or whenever any of the children misbehaved, a particular child, Eva (the client), was seen as the bad kid. When she was accused of misbehaving and was aware that she had not misbehaved, Eva would get upset. This would be further used by the family to show Eva that her behavior in the "upset state" was proof of her guilt. Thus, Eva's upset reaction was connected to guilt, and as she grew to adulthood, she continued to equate her psychological pain to rejection and inferiority. However in cases such as Eva's, the parents or the chief caretakers *are* actually the guilty parties because the child is their passive victim who has taken on the responsibility of bearing the family's burdens.

Because pain is equated with not being well, the clients

often say that they would like to be normal, which simply means that they do not understand that all people can feel pain, although they may still be healthy people. Although scapegoated people's thoughts, feelings, intentions, and words are overlooked or discounted—as if they are not human beings—their behavior and motives are evaluated and used. Thus, they are left with an abundant failure to recognize their own self or identity. Scapegoats are constricted in their development because at a very young age they learn to adapt to the family ethos. If they do not, they believe that other people as well as their family will look down on them (Fossum & Mason, 1986).

Shame

Guilt can also be explained as the self-blame that a person endures and suffers for breaking a moral code, whereas shame is the inner experience of being looked down upon by a group. Fossum and Mason (1986) explain that shame, like pride, is related to the public image of oneself rather than one's actual behavior. Shame and pride are interrelated in family situations. Pride and shame prevent one from establishing his or her personhood. That is, the family system on the shame end of the continuum shares with its members vague and distorted personal boundary definitions that inhibit the development of a mature self, and this is particularly true of the scapegoated child.

The scapegoated person can be compared to the whipping boy who had to take whippings on behalf of the young prince who, by universal acknowledgment, was said not to have any defects in his personality. Thus, when the whipping boy was whipped because the young prince had done something wrong, the punishment was used to help the prince understand that he was not really perfect and face the shame of violation of the nation's illusion about his own image. Although the prince might have felt the shame if he were sensitive, he still did not feel the pain that the whipping boy endured. In a scapegoating family, the targeted child takes on the pain as well as the shame.

Ego Structures

The ego structures of scapegoated people are fragile and also distant from others. When they are constantly made to feel guilty and their reactions are negated repeatedly, they learn to develop a negative reaction to their own affect and sensitivity because doors have been opened to feeling more guilt and pain.

One 22-year-old client always dressed severely, undermining her sexuality with baggy pants and blouses that fit to suppress her already small breasts. She cut her hair short and wore absolutely no makeup. In short, she looked like a boy. To discuss her femininity was painful—the result of sexual abuse by her father. However, her father had always told her that it was their little secret and made her feel responsible for his behavior. At this point in her life, it was obvious that the pain and guilt she had experienced led to some degree of splitting and denial in her personality. This allowed her to automatically evade the experience.

As discussed earlier, the ego is able to split the internal perception of the relationship of objects to one another, or it can experience self as being split or fragmented by a force believed to be within or beyond self. Defensively speaking, there are passive and active ways of splitting. Active splitting of the object and self is intentional, whether conscious or unconscious, whereas passive splitting just seems to happen through the experience of fragmentational confrontation with an overwhelming reality. The oppressively scapegoated person experiences more passive splitting as he or she is constantly overwhelmed with a sense of personal unworthiness.

Negative Body Image

As mentioned earlier another manner of suffering for scapegoats is that they view themselves in the most negative light; this often involves negative body image. Scapegoated Randy, a weak, mild, and tormented 11-year-old, blurted out in therapy that he was not only troublesome, but also ugly to look at: he thought he was small, puny, and had an ugly nose, just like everyone at home had always told him.

Some of the feelings scapegoated persons have experienced in terms of themselves and their bodies become apparent when the scapegoated person stiffens or tells another not to touch him or her if touched.

While I was working with Justin, an abused child, I touched his shoulder to show my approval of how well he had conducted himself in the playground. As soon as I did this, his behavior changed. He reacted angrily, pulled away from me, and told me never to touch him for any reason. This eight-year-old exhibited so much anger and apparently experienced so much pain from a simple touch that he probably considered himself an "untouchable" person.

Edward had been scapegoated during the eight years

he lived at home. He had been punched and kicked and told over and over again that he was unworthy of any love or recognition. All he had experienced as far as he could remember was the agony of physical and mental pain, and he viewed himself as extremely ugly. Edward was almost armored against feeling anything positive about himself. When I commented that he had dressed "really sharp," he would look at me as if I were tormenting him. Edward had learned to devalue himself to such an extent that he could not possibly accept any compliment.

As specified, the scapegoated person develops a great capacity for bearing other people's pain. With intense therapeutic help the scapegoated person can learn to develop a positive attitude toward herself or himself and then begin to develop a shared sense of suffering with the scapegoater, who also has unresolved issues.

Separation-Individuation

Many times, the relentlessly scapegoated person has extreme difficulty in separating and individuating from the family of origin. As Edward, Ruskin, and Turrini (1981) say, separation-individuation takes place on two tracks. Separation refers to the child's movements away from the fusion with the mother, and individuation includes those steps that lead to the development of an individual's personal and unique qualities. When negotiation of the separation-individuation subphases—differentiation, practicing, rapprochement, and object constancy —takes place favorably, the child grows up to be healthy; he or she moves from autism, which is the tendency to view life in terms of one's own needs and desires, unmindful of objective reality, to mutually beneficial symbiosis, which is when mother and child live together in an amicable relationship.

However, when there is no optimum symbiosis and basic trust where the child is affected, then the child will be ill-prepared for the discovery of the other-than-mother (chief caretaker) world (Edward, Ruskin, & Turrini, 1981). The scapegoated client who has not been brought up with beneficial nurturing needs to be provided with a safe container—a totally safe and congenial atmosphere in therapy—in order to view the rejections and abuses and to deal with them accordingly. This will be discussed further in Chapter 4.

PROBLEMS OF ASSERTION IN SCAPEGOATED PERSONS

Some parents envy the scapegoated child for the strengths they perceive in him or her. This envy is directed toward making the child become a perfect person and reach standards that are stringently high. The scapegoat is viewed as having a degree of control and power that, in reality, he or she does not feel. Therefore, these parents spend their time suppressing the child in relation to his or her assertiveness or dependency. When children are constantly controlled and made to feel that they should not have a will of their own, they begin to believe that this is true, and slowly but steadily their instincts to be assertive disappear. This disappearance happens when there is a devaluation of the instinctual appetites and affects and personal sensitivities and rhythms by the predominant adults to whom the child is intensely exposed to (Perera, 1986). Moreover, the extremely high standards set by the parents are impossible for the child to live up to, and this causes the child to feel worthless, useless, and guilty. In therapy scapegoated persons have to work very hard to develop their assertive powers.

Negation of Needs

Many scapegoated children learn to negate their own needs. They also learn that to say "No" brings on the wrath of the parent. For instance, a child who was allergic to oranges was forced to eat oranges, but he was criticized as a spoiled child and fussy eater if he refused. This action violated his self-protective instincts, but he would give in to his parents and become sicker as he ate the oranges. If he resisted in any way, his parents viewed this as bad. To live up to the unrealistic standards the parents set for him, the child learned to eat everything they gave him. Thus, he turned all his pain with food into blame and self-hate.

Aggression

Scapegoated children also grow up not understanding the parental aggression that they face. Their parents do not help them to understand the differences between assertiveness and aggression as a necessary function of the ego. Both assertiveness and aggression are punished, leaving the child with a sense of failure and guilt. When these scapegoated children do show anger, it takes the form of impulsive, often violent, outbursts against almost anyone. Often, as seen among the scapegoated:

> Twelve-year-old Matt was very angry with his therapist because of the content of the interview, so he walked out of her office in a rage and

kicked a young secretarial staff member. Matt's outburst was really unexpected as he had always been a mild child who usually had trouble talking about his problems. Matt was overwhelmed by a sense of remorse and guilt, yet because the outburst was sudden and unplanned, he did not feel any responsibility for this unacceptable behavior.

The Split Self

As mentioned earlier, often the child whose ego strengths have been rigidly damaged learns to split the self. How does this happen? Take the case of Brenda:

Brenda is an adult survivor of sexual abuse by her uncle (father's brother) with whom she lived from the age of five. Her father was aware of the abuse but viewed it as something that a daughter had to undergo in the family. As a young girl, Brenda had all kinds of instruments thrust into her body at various times in her life. When she was nine, her vagina split open due to the thrusting of some object and she was admitted into a hospital. However, the injury was defined as self-inflicted and incest was not suspected; there was not much suspicion about incest in those days.

Today Brenda, a grown woman in therapy, is attempting to work through her anger and pain. She explained how she dealt with her own psychic split. Brenda said that when her uncle took her to the bedroom she learned to split herself. She would leave her self at the bottom of the stairs and take only her body—which she felt that she did not own—to the bedroom upstairs.

As mentioned earlier, splitting can be broadly described as a basic mental mechanism in which perceptual, cognitive, and defense operations are included. This is considered to be a universal experience of human beings and originates from the experience of existing in separate subselves or separate personalities, which have never been unified into a single one. The experience of being split is more common among abnormal personalities who have not achieved a confident capacity to repress. This is also another way of stating that those who have not achieved a normal resolution of the oedipus complex, with the legacy of a normal superego and the capacity for normal repression, will experience a split to a greater degree. Individuals who have achieved normal repression as a result of oedipus complex resolution will experience unconscious splitting but will not have a conscious experience of it. Normal people can also be split, but their experience of splitting is mitigated by repression (Grotstein, 1985).

Veiling

Many scapegoated people also learn to use veiling. Veiling can be described as a series of passive-aggressive distortions and maneuvers which allow for some expression of split-off impulses, but this expression is indirect and usually unconscious. These innocently hostile people suffer from a need for cold vengeance, which turns into spite toward one's own self. They are, however, enslaved to the scapegoater with a generalized fatalistic sense of doom. Such people have their aggressive impulses split off but also turned toward their own victim-ego self-destructively, and they spend their whole life totally dependent on placating the accusing scapegoater (Perera, 1986).

Baiting

Perera uses the term baiting to define a safely veiled expression of the individual's own anger to provoke another person. One young scapegoated woman indicated, "To be in control of feelings is to be strong and superior. When the other person goes out of control, I watch and secretly gloat. It's a tactic of being a bitch. I'm deliberately vicious, but so cold-bloodedly and virtuously, it makes the other person want to strangle himself. No one knows I hate myself completely."

This woman had moved from a position of generalized fatalistic doom and was beginning to enjoy her own assertiveness, which had been absent all these years. Baiting others enabled her to learn to feel better about herself. Getting angry at others, which she had not previously been able to do, is meaningful for this person. Because the ego is not completely broken, this anger gives the scapegoated person permission to defend himself or herself (Perera, 1986).

Coldness

Another way of dealing with the feelings of being the one at the bottom of the totem pole takes a form of assertion called coldness. When scapegoated persons feel that they are not being treated right, they take their revenge by being very cold to everyone with whom they come in contact. The coldness allows the scapegoat to protect himself or herself from the retaliation that could occur when the other person responds (Perera, 1986).

Difficulty in bearing pain is seen in the masks that the person creates for himself or herself. The victim usually suffers from helpless rage and this, in turn, creates a kind of hostility and a subtle thwarting of others.

Self-punitive Assertion

Often such people see themselves as "poor me" and at times hurt or punish themselves with the hope that the other person will look out for them. Behind all these maneuvers to hurt oneself are hopes that if one hurts or punishes oneself enough, then others will be good to him or her.

Ryan, a 16-year-old boy, used to get hurt every time he went out. He was labeled masochistic as he allowed others to beat him up. When he was hurt, he hoped that he could win the sympathy and care of other people, particularly his adult caretakers.

It can be explained that among the scapegoated there is a lack of separation between themselves and the scapegoaters. They are highly fused with the scapegoaters, and almost a magical level of consciousness exists between the scapegoater and the scapegoated. Because the scapegoater is very powerful, the individual consciousness of the scapegoated has not emerged out of the level of the body-self (Perera, 1986).

For clients who combine self-destruction and spiteful assertion and who have lost the instinct for self-defense, it is important early in therapy to objectify the sadistic or punishing parent. Otherwise the client develops self-punitive assertive behaviors; the result is masochistic behavior that is turned toward the client's body in the form of impulsive, self-punitive acts (Perera, 1986). The second root of self-punitive assertion is self-preserving habit, for spitefulness is the way in which these children learn to survive. In this case, aggression is turned against both the rejector and the self. With all their hateful spite there is an intense desire to survive. The spite that these people feel hides the hurt of alienation and the lack of someone to meet their own dependency needs. In this manner scapegoated children refuse to take in reactions or responses that are painful and poisonous to bear.

For example when a child is focused on candy, torment occurs when candy is placed within her reach, but she is not allowed to take it. So the little girl grows up believing that she does not deserve any sweets in life. Later on, this child might move toward becoming like a punitive parent, refusing to eat.

For therapy to be successful, many techniques have to be used. Assertion and building up self-esteem become very important for the functioning of this type of client. Silent intense visualizations of assertions or assertive actions in therapy sessions are useful. One of the major tasks of therapy is to make this person aware that assertion is good and to validate this assertiveness constantly.

NEED, DEMAND, AND DEPENDENCY

In some scapegoated people desire is spoiled, devalued, and repressed. Teaching these people open assertion, a form of wanting for themselves, is almost impossible initially because they are used to being demanded upon by others, and utilize behaviors that undermine and inhibit gratification. Some of these behaviors are shown as disguised requests, negated requests, and so forth. For example, one form of need gratification of the scapegoated person is compulsive caretaking of others, that is, a satisfaction of the instinct in projection.

Unfulfilled Needs

As scapegoats' needs are not fulfilled, they tend to become victims of both split-off and negative impulsives and the negative judgments that have been made of them. At other times, scapegoated people experience hidden and projected dependency. This dependency is often coupled with a growing fear that accompanies secret rage and resentment. In scapegoated people demand and dependency are usually split off. The repressed demand says "I want what I want" in a primitive, arrogant, and greedy manner and functions as a hidden assumption that the world owes it to the scapegoated person for being the burden-bearer and the caretaker of his or her family or the representative of the collective group of scapegoated individuals.

Such people are very demanding. One woman told me in therapy, "You have to do this for me. If not, I will hurt myself." A person's identity is often weakened by identification with both the prince and the pauper. The prince being the family whose desires she had fulfilled until this point and the pauper is herself whose desires she is not sure she could fulfill. In these situations, the therapist has to function in the role of caring person.

Concrete and Symbolic Fulfillment

Sometimes dependency needs may require concrete and symbolic fulfillment. Though clients may desire a hug, a kiss, or a compliment, they are afraid to present or talk about their own needs because they have only fulfilled other people's needs for a long period of time. One of therapy's first objectives is to work through the scapegoated person's denial of his or her own needs and wishes.

At some point in therapy scapegoated people may insist that the therapist or another person fulfill their demands. Usually such stubbornness is a revelation of the developing capacity to become assertive. In order to deal with these demands, it is necessary for the ego to become active and responsible in pursuit of needs. While dealing with a scapegoated person, the therapist should view the demands as a positive sign that the person is moving toward his or her own development and the satisfaction of his or her own needs. The demands being made on the therapist by the person who is attempting to develop his or her own ego strengths should be viewed patiently, for there will come a time when the self-discipline of the scapegoated person is sufficient to restrain his or her own unleashed greed and/or rage.

At times, people have learned to connect discipline with punishment and shame. Here the therapist has to help move this client's instinct from that of accustomed concreteness to symbolic satisfaction of the individual's own needs. The therapist should help this client close the split between masochistic self-sacrifice and arrogant and impulsive demands.

The satisfaction of even small desires is an intoxicating

experience for the scapegoat because until that time the scapegoat's own needs had been subjugated to the needs of others. The person has to develop a balance between claiming and giving.

This may not be easy to accomplish. There are some clients who are so full of self-hatred that when they meet their own needs, the gratification may threaten their self-image as people who are not entitled to get any satisfaction or pleasure out of life because of an indebtedness similar to enslavement. Therefore, they fall back on old arguments and blame each time they face acceptance because of the fear that the acceptance is not deserved and could be short-lived (Perera, 1986). For such clients it is important to develop a positive transference so that they can accept the unconditional caring that is provided them and use it to help their own growth and development over a period of time.

In the following chapter, there will be a further discussion of the healing process. Accuser-victim aspects of the scapegoated, negative self-image, projective identification, disidentification, development of a sense of identity, and the therapeutic process will be presented.

4

The Healing Process

For the scapegoated person the healing process depends on what has been worked through and to what extent while the person is dealing with his or her issues. The process is a long one: the scapegoat must learn to disidentify from an accustomed or lifelong role. To implement the goal of unhooking, the therapist should take into consideration the specific style, developmental level, individual psychological configuration, and openness to change of the client. In therapy there ultimately occurs the client's discovery of himself or herself in relation to others, family, and society and the validation of the person as a whole, a process that encompasses working with and bringing together the oppositions (the victim and the accuser) within the scapegoated person.

DISUNITY OF SELF

As discussed earlier, scapegoated persons tend to take the blame of others on themselves and become self-blaming, for somewhere within themselves they feel their own guilt in the family situation. But learning to connect to the real self comes slowly to provide a safe matrix that relieves the person of the need to be a perfectionist and the desire to take on everyone's faults.

Before we proceed further let me distinguish between the real self and the ego. The ego performs a number of functions that can be classified as perceptive, cognitive, adaptive, protective, executive, and integrative. The ego's perceptive functions include perception of self based on self-awareness, self-image, and body-image and perception of others in relation to self and reality testing. The real self can be seen in the intrapsychic sense of the sum of self and objective representations with their related affects. The term "real" is synonymous with healthy or normal. The representations of the real self have an important conscious reality component even though unconscious fantasy elements occur. Masterson emphasizes that the real self has a function in reality as well as feeling real. Masterson, in discussing the real self, describes it using Erikson's (Erikson, 1968) personal identity aspect of Erikson's concept of identity rather than ego identity (Erikson, 1968). As Masterson (1985) indicates, the real self emerges in early intrapsychic development and grows through early childhood and adolescence; then in adulthood it must be articulated in reality.

In the severely scapegoated person, however, this maturation process is not completed. Usually the real self exists as a parallel partner of the ego, having its own development and its own capacities; the self and the ego develop and function together in tandem, like two horses in the same harness. If the ego is arrested in its development, then it can be said that the self is likewise arrested. One does not see an arrested ego without an arrested self. In this respect, the self is viewed as the representational arm of the ego. Similarly, the ego in its dealings with volition and will, and with the activation and gratification of individual wishes, is the executive arm of the self. However, the primary function of the ego is to maintain intrapsychic balance (Masterson, 1985).

Accuser-Victim Split

The fundamental function of the therapist is to help the scapegoated client deal with and work with reality. The aim is to help the person move from a split sense of self to a whole self. As mentioned earlier, the two aspects of that split are the accuser and the hidden victim. The accuser half of the ego is alienated and shadow-bearing. The hidden victim is the portion of the ego in which the scapegoated person experiences exile, feeling the un-healed wounds and grieving both for himself or herself and for the family members who did the scapegoating. The scapegoated person has to be helped to achieve a wholeness that contains an enduring, asserting, desiring self, conscious of functioning for itself as a person.

The first step toward healing takes place in the atmo-sphere of blamelessness that characterizes the therapeutic setting. The therapist must be sensitive to the needs of the client; for the client who is nurtured in the healing process becomes willing to risk change and to play with various possibilities in his or her life. Through a positive relationship in therapy, the client feels able to express all kinds of concerns, without being blamed, in the totally congenial and unconditionally accepting environment of the therapist's presence. The therapist helps the client to present the different sides of his or her personality. Through constant dialogue between the split aspects, the person learns to own the negative side and to recognize the existence of the positive side. With intense understanding, acceptance, and objectivity, the therapist can help the scapegoated person learn to accept the positive side and eventually to use it for his or her own benefit.

George (see Chapter 5), an adolescent boy who had his lips burned on the stove, showed steady progress when he was met consistently with support and humor by his therapist. He loved to laugh, and so the therapist used her humor to reach him. Although his laughter was usually used to disrupt people's discussions and could be a source of distraction and interruption, with help he was able to use laughter in a different way. For the first time in his life, George found that his humor was worthwhile and learned to use it positively. Another area in which his growth was encouraged was in his guitar playing. He was eager to improve his skill as a way of relating to his older brother, Peter. Peter, who lived away from home, was supportive of George's desires.

The more George's growth was fostered and his energies channeled into positive activities, the more constructive and disciplined he grew. The therapist helped George to see the positive side of his own self, which George had not recognized earlier but which he was slowly learning to accept and to live with. Through a process that was extremely painful, including a home visit, George learned to view his family as being dysfunctional and to accept the fact that his parents had their own issues in which he was too often caught.

Particularly with reference to his mother, George learned to accept her as being limited. He gave up his intense desire to live with her at home, as he realized she had serious problems of her own. There were many attempts, some successful, to help him create his own boundaries of self-definition.

Boundaries

For scapegoated people it is important to create a link between the past and the present: between seeing themselves as nonfamily and seeing their role in the family of origin. Even though scapegoated people take on the responsibility for their family's desires and needs, they view themselves as being distinctly different from the rest of the family—indeed, as nonfamily. An important aspect of the healing process involves acknowledging this self-view as nonfamily followed by making connections between the act of scapegoating a child and the dynamics within the family of origin.

In the beginning stages of therapy, a crucial element is the alliance between therapist and client establishing the connection between the client's own issues and those assigned by family. Properly timed attempts to help the client view the family as it really is further that objective. The family of the scapegoated person commonly reveals enmeshed boundaries: there is an abundance of togetherness, but not necessarily of a positive nature. All members are locked together, and one or more of the members do not develop their own separate selves within the family group. The parents' sense of self-identity determines to a large extent the type of boundaries with which they are comfortable. In many families of severely scapegoated children, their sense of identity as a family has not been crystallized into a functional one, and this nuclear family suffers in many ways.

One of the purposes in therapy is to support the victim-ego of the scapegoated person and to work toward disarming and dissolving, through careful confrontation, the defenses of the alienated accuser ego, which finds fault with everything it does. Scapegoated clients are usually very defensive, fearful of letting go of the defenses that have served them for so long. Their sole conscious identity is often completely connected to their own defenses. As one 10-year-old blurted out to his therapist, "I am a sick, poor, crazy bastard." He was diabetic; his grandfather who was his legal guardian was on welfare. He was severely scapegoated and was illegitimate. His words clearly reflected his self-image. But as clients gain the ability to handle their emotions sensibly, those irrationally defensive emotions are walled off. Clients begin to feel a proud but uneasy strength when this rigid defensiveness falls away.

Loneliness

Before they can get themselves together, clients who have begun to shed their defenses are often overcome by a numbing depression. Symptoms include sleep disturbances, appetite disorders, decreased sexual interest, loss of interest in ordinarily pleasurable activities, self-reproach, thoughts of death and suicide, and vague somatic complaints. Many such clients will admit they suffer from hopeless, helpless despair (Doherty & Baird, 1983), underlined by confusion and intense loneliness. This loneliness, almost to a point of desperation, relates to a feeling of abandonment—the sense that someone important is missing, even when living members of the family are available. Lonely persons often are viewed as family outsiders.

There are at least three factors that prolong loneliness. They are unresolved grief, pathological certainty, and parental abdication (Large, 1989). Unresolved grief persists in scapegoated families, where a sense of loss combines with a feeling of emptiness and anger. Pathological certainty, unremitting and relentless, weighs the child down with a negative self-image based on the parents' conviction. For example, one boy was constantly referred to as being the black sheep and was told that nothing good will come out of him, until he came to believe this without any doubt. When family abdication occurs, as it commonly does in the homes of scapegoated children, a parent prematurely gives up the parenting role; someone in the next generation is then predisposed to loneliness (Large, 1989).

FEAR, RAGE, AND PAIN

Along with loneliness, the scapegoated person also suffers from fear and rage. In therapy clients need to be assured that the therapist will be there to provide emotional and practical support. Laing (1965) asserts that the "internalized" family, which is constructed during the early years of a child's life, represents the embodiment of relations and operations between elements and sets of elements. The elements could be objects, introjected or external. The family provides patterns that are habitually used to ascribe relations between objects. Normally these patterns shape our reality images. Laing refers to this as the "family map." The person projects this map onto the family and carries it over to other situations. It is no simple set of introjected objects, but more a matrix for dramas and patterns of space-time sequences to be enacted.

This shows how much effort and patience is required by the therapist to work with these kinds of clients. The clients need to move away from original ways of thinking and patterns of behavior, because now they are self-destructive. They slowly and steadily learn to discriminate between pain that is their own and the pain of others that they have learned to endure. As the wounds start to heal, their hidden or damaged ego begins to develop. Slowly they learn to see and to be seen objectively. Scapegoated persons also learn that desire, action, and pain can be experienced without being branded or branding themselves. Usually such acceptance and objectivity are themselves psychologically nourishing and provide a wholesome container where the growing self can learn to endure frustration, to assert, and to accept both dependency and independence. As one client put it,

> *"I wasn't sure you liked me until I started to see myself as a whole person with goodness and strengths and not just a bad and guilty person. I feel whole and complete and you see all parts of me and not just my ugly fragments that I now realize are the different parts of me and I like myself . . . at last."*

Thus, slowly the person realizes that there are inner allies that are objective, protective, and respectful. These represent the slow and difficult process of healing.

NEGATIVE SELF-IMAGE

Self-hatred and Guilt

The idealization of the parent or caretaker who leaves the child feeling empty sets the stage for the child's loss of positive self-identity. While growing up, the child faces a system of negative thoughts, feelings, and attitudes that is an integral part of the emotional environment. Severely scapegoated people do not learn self-hatred in adulthood; it is fostered in their person as a child. Oftentimes in therapy these children show a strong and seemingly perverse need to hang onto their self-hatreds and their tendency toward self-denial and destruction, and they adamantly refuse to change a negative image. What purpose does it serve? Maintaining a negative self-image protects the person against intrusions into fantasies in which the person predicts rejection by others and, on a deeper level, sees and experiences himself or herself as unlovable. The fantasies about rejection serve as safeguards against close personal relationships. The person does not want to take a chance on being hurt and on being hurt again and again; therefore it is easier to cling to feelings of worthlessness.

Unfortunately, the negative self-image is consistent with the parent's or caretaker's definition of the person who accepts the parental negative image. In order to change, the scapegoated person has to work through the negative self-image and negative self-evaluations that cause anxiety and pain. This goal implies that the person must break free of the oppressive bond of the family, which—through the image of the powerful, all-knowing parents—interferes with the process of gratifying the self. But this becomes ery difficult when the parents are themselves children who cannot separate themselves from their own parents. Quite often, the severely scapegoated child's parents are infantile in some ways, and that is the reason why they use their child as a scapegoat.

Anxiety

In therapy the person has to face a great deal of anxiety; without it, no therapeutic change can happen. Goodwin (1987) defines anxiety as an emotion that signifies the presence of a danger that cannot be identified or, if identified, is not sufficiently threatening to justify the intensity of emotion. Many times, the true source of distress is unknown. As Goodwin puts it, "Anxiety is an itch that can't be scratched because it is about two inches left of your third thoracic vertebra—no, down a little, up slightly . . . yes, no . . . damn!" (Goodwin, 1987, p. 3).

Anxiety is distinct from fear. Fear is a response to the presence of a known danger. The strength of fear is more or less proportionate to the degree of danger. Fear is a useful emotion because it steers one away from danger. In contrast, even though anxious people think they know what they are afraid of—whether a dog, cat or a garden snake, or a rebuke from a boss—the real source of distress is unknown. They may even recognize that their anxiety is disproportionate to the threat.

But not all anxiety is bad; some degree of anxiety is good for us, adding zest to our lives and keeping us on our toes. It may build character, enhance creativity, and enlarge awareness of life's possibilities. Anxiety like this is called normal anxiety. The kind of anxiety a seriously scapegoated person feels is abnormally severe and characterized by uncertainty and helplessness. Certain questions are likely to bother this person intensely: Do my parents approve of my being in therapy? Will my parents come into therapy to work at some of the family issues? Chronic unresolved life conflicts also create a large share of the person's anxiety.

Self-identity

Besides confronting their anxiety, scapegoated clients need to work at changing their own self-identity to which they have been accustomed for a long time. The contradiction between their old and new conceptions of reality often leaves them with a temporarily unstable sense of identity. All their lives they have harbored some well-defined thoughts of the self as being unlovable that, though painful, have served to provide a self-identity. It takes a number of events to bring about positive changes in the clients' self-concept, but they are strenuously avoided because of the anxiety that the perceived loss entails (Firestone, 1985).

Twelve-year-old Allen had been involved in fights with other children in school. He had also been constantly mistreated at home and bore the brunt of all family problems. However, through strenuous therapy he learned to understand that he possessed some qualities that could be highly valued; for instance, his ability to study and his skill at playing football. However, Allen habitually downplayed these strengths. Perhaps unconsciously he saw them as a way out of his role of scapegoat in the family. So he did everything possible to sabotage his newly constructed positive self-image, because he was more easily accepted by his family when he played the "bad kid." Therapy in this case required seeing the family, too, although they were very reluctant and saw Allen's behavior solely as his problem.

Children like Allen have feelings of worthlessness, self-accusatory thoughts, and very erratic mood swings, which are controlled by internal negative thought processes or inner dialogue, which Firestone refers to as the "voice." The voice is seen to represent the introjection of the parents' rejecting attitudes toward the child, both spoken and unspoken. Firestone describes the "voice" as the language of an insidious self-destructive process existing to varying degrees in every person. The voice represents an external point of view initially derived from caretakers' or parents' suppressed hostile feelings toward the child. In scapegoated persons, the voice is loud, unanswerable, and consistently negative. These people suffer from self-castigation, guilt, and distortion of self, addressing themselves in such terms as, "why did you do that you dimwit?" They torment themselves about their life situations and problems. Their self-critical thoughts echo what they have been told by their parents, representing them as unlovable, worthless, and bad. Thus it preserves the "bad child" image. The clients come to believe this message and see themselves as unlovable persons, rather than perceiving the parents as being rejecting or inadequate.

As will be seen in the Walker family (Chapter 5), the mother was inadequate and did not wish to hug her son, Leo, which he first interpreted as rejection, but in therapy he learned to understand it as his mother's own issue, where she was a victim of destructive entitlement. However, in many situations, the internal environments that scapegoats create for themselves serve to promote and sustain the defensive process by interpreting reality in such a way that the scapegoat's negative self-image is preserved and the parental misconceptions of the scapegoat are reinforced.

Negative Parental Attitudes

When a parent taunts, ridicules, belittles, reprimands, and punishes a child about the way he or she looks or acts, the child learns to internalize that attitude which is then carried to other areas of his or her behavior. The child begins to self-attack in all areas and thus develops a global negative attitude toward self. These generalized self-attacks are commonly accompanied by agitation, irritability, and a slightly depressed mood. Many scapegoated individuals have a system of misconceptions and negative attitudes about themselves. The voice is a part of the self-destructive process, not functioning as an expression of a positive system of values but always promoting self-attack and castigation.

Internalization of negative parental attitudes prevents these children from gradually developing their own internal set of standards and thus necessitates the adoption of an external value system. They are taught to subscribe to an external system of values. First as children and later as adults, they act from a motivation to avoid punishment by authorities rather than reflect a compassionate attitude toward themselves and their fellow beings (Firestone, 1985). People who grow up with a voice that encourages denial of self are not only self-sacrificing, but also self-destructive.

How does the negative self-attitude begin? Suppose a child was told over and over again that she or he is unattractive. By outside standards, the child may be attractive enough—perhaps even good-looking—but this fact is overlooked by both the family and the child. These children will usually be self-conscious about their clothes and hair but do nothing to enhance their appearance; having learned to assume that they are ugly.

Many scapegoated persons believe their own self-attacks and are predisposed to behavior that, in turn, eventually causes their negative traits to become a major part of their style and approach to life. In this manner children incorporate the adults' distorted definitions of them and later use them to categorize themselves negatively.

While working with disturbed children in an agency, I saw a young adolescent boy running down the hall toward my office. He flung the door open and screamed, "So, you are the new counselor!" Without another word, he slammed my door shut. After the third repetition of this performance, I decided to call him back and talk to him. It took some effort just to persuade him to come back. I looked at him as he stood before me, poised to run, and simply asked, "Why are you slamming the door?" To my sorrow, he burst into laughter. "You oughta know better," he jeered. "All of us guys are crazy. All the other counselors know what to expect!" Those who routinely accepted their bad behavior had perhaps contributed to the negative spiral escalating in the lives of these youngsters.

Origins of the Negative Self-image

Children's negative self-image gets its start early in life as a result of their suffering from emotional deprivation in the family. Parents' overt or covert rejection of the child affects the child's self-esteem. Though the child's feeling of self-hatred and depressive states multiply as the child grows older, they are basically the result of the caretakers' or parents' deeply repressed desire to destroy the aliveness and spontaneity of the child whenever the child intrudes on their defenses. These hostile wishes and destructive urges influence the child's self-concept perhaps more than the parental inadequacies or lack of love. In response, the child attempts to move toward self-destruction.

The parent's unconscious desire to quiet the child or suppress the child's feelings arise because the parent is defended and emotionally deadened and does not wish to be awakened from this cut-off state by tender feelings toward his or her offspring (Firestone, 1985). The parent works at preventing his or her own repressed pain from coming to the surface. The child's spontaneous feelings are suppressed and supplanted by socially designated feelings, and the defenses of the parent prevent the child from expressing the unwanted stimulation of repressed feelings. The more defended the parent is and the more rigid the system of defense toward the child, the more hostility there is toward the child, who is really an innocent intruder. The child feels the parent's anger and with it the negative parental attitude already internalized, turning it against the self in a form of self-hatred. Many scape-goated children have usually internalized everything to such a degree that they think they are bad and they support their parents in being punitive toward them. Firestone (1985) indicates that the child's pain, humiliation, and fear are repressed also and feelings are blamed on oneself for real or imagined wrongdoing taking place.

Similarly, they do not express the anger they feel toward the parent. Anger can be defined as a strong feeling of displeasure and belligerence aroused by a real or supposed wrong; further it can be described as a sudden violent displeasure accompanied by a desire to retaliate (Webster, 1989). But since children are afraid to retaliate against parents, the anger is turned against themselves as self-hatred and/or depression.

To struggle against these self-destructive forces is very painful. Scapegoated children usually have such low self-esteem that they cannot answer the voice with positive, realistic statements about themselves.

Negative Traits of the Parents

Parental qualities can contribute to the child's formation of a negative self-concept, causing the child to feel guilty and self-hating. Many parents who deny undesirable traits in themselves project those traits onto their children and then punish them for possessing those qualities, whether imagined or real. These children become, in effect, the dumping ground for qualities the parents hate in themselves. They learn to see themselves through the parents' eyes and see their behavior as entirely justified.

> Sixteen-year-old Vicky was ill-treated by her parents from the age of five, more overtly by her father than by her mother. She could sense when her father wanted to physically abuse her. Many times, the abuse occurred for little or no reason, usually as a carryover of problems in the workplace or of tensions within the family. The father would take everything out on this particular child. No matter what went wrong in the family or who did what, Vicky would get punished. She learned to internalize and see herself as bad. At 16, she

was the mother of a one-year-old son whom she started to abuse, "as he did not obey her." She reflected her parents' behavior and in therapy she justified her own behavior by saying, insightfully, "nobody expected any better from me."

Many children take on the characteristics of a punishing parent in order to relieve anxiety and gain some measure of security. Human beings are capable of incorporating into themselves an image of their parents as the parents were in the past, when they hated and feared them the most as when they were children (Firestone, 1985).

Sixteen-year-old Betty was difficult to control, had constant temper tantrums, and had become pregnant for the second time. Although Betty had been informed about contraceptives and had been provided with them, she refused to take them on a regular basis. Repeatedly confronted by the therapist, Betty responded that her mother had done the same and that she did not see what was wrong with her behavior. She then broke into a temper tantrum that lasted for five minutes. Her temper tantrums also called to mind the behavior of her mother who had three illegitimate children and frequently flew off the handle when anyone irritated her.

By internalizing a negative self-concept, a person is likely to behave in ways that perpetuate it.

Twenty-six-year-old Sandra spent all her time shopping for clothes and makeup that she hardly used. Scapegoated at home from a young age, she possessed a great deal of anger, which came out in her attitude toward her shopping sprees. Though she ran out of room to store her purchases, she still felt the need to buy more clothes. And though she began to have financial difficulties, falling several months behind in paying her bills, she could not seem to curb her spending. In time, it became apparent that her habits succeeded in getting her into constant trouble, which she was used to when she lived with her parents.

Until Sandra's anger from the abuse and scapegoating come to the surface, she will not be ready to work on her other issues.

Resistance to Changing the Negative Self-image

Scapegoated persons have to be challenged to examine their own negative images of themselves. When clients start to identify their self-attacks, then comes acceptance of their own behavior. This is the inception of therapy—when the person begins to move away from the scapegoated role and views growth as positive.

This is also the beginning of the child's separation from the internalized parent. The client has to divest himself or herself of the qualities that belong to the parent and recognize the parent's nature for what it is. This step can cause the client a lot of pain and guilt and thus may trigger resistance at some crucial point in therapy. Having accepted the negative image, and fearing the unknown, the client could become extremely stubborn and resistant in changing his or her role image. Challenging a person's negative self-image and self-hatred also means commencing to help the client cope with tension and anxiety.

Curtis got himself into trouble without any effort. He had been beaten, starved, and tied to his crib until he was three years of age. When he cried out of hunger, he was called a troublemaker. At eight he was abandoned. He was placed in a series of foster homes, but he did not fare well in them and was abused, including sexual abuse in two of the homes. At 14, Curtis had a knack for getting into trouble. He would abuse his friends verbally and consequently would be physically attacked. He was so regularly beaten by other boys that I had never seen him without a bruise showing on his face, neck, or arms. Curtis saw himself as a useless, worthless person. Somewhere, deep inside, he felt that he deserved all the abuse. Although it was his mother who had abandoned him, he felt guilty and believed that he should have tried harder to help her, even as an eight-year-old.

In therapy, he had tried his utmost to provoke me, calling me names and seemingly daring me to be nice to him. Throughout, I was patient but firm with him. One day, while playing with seven other boys in a group, Curtis got attacked for cursing at two of them. I witnessed the incident and noticed that Curtis had not been the one to start the name-calling; however, he fell very quickly into the role of the scapegoat and had the other children pushing and hitting him. Feeling angry and frustrated, I intervened. As I stopped the taunting and the shoving, Curtis stared at me with amazement. Nobody had ever supported him in such a difficult situation. In this setting, it had been accepted that he would be playing the scapegoat, just as he had done as a child.

That evening, as I approached my car in the dark parking lot, I heard someone call my name. The tall, lanky figure of Curtis emerged from the gloom and stood by my car, his hands stuffed awkwardly in his jean pockets. He kicked at an invisible pebble on the blacktop. "I don't know why you did it," he mumbled, "but anyway, thank you."

Suddenly, for me, starbursts lit up the sky. This was it—the breaking point of his scapegoating and the beginning of serious therapy work. The road was not smooth from there: at first he kept trying to slip back into the old role as scapegoat of the agency, and there were setbacks. However, with support, Curtis accomplished dramatic changes in his behavior as he tried to learn and accept himself as a good person who deserved to be treated with dignity.

PROJECTIVE IDENTIFICATION

As mentioned earlier, parents of scapegoated children use a mental mechanism known as projective identification to get rid of unwanted parts of themselves. Projective identification has positive uses, such as vicarious introspection, and in its sublimated forms, it is used for empathy; but in the scapegoating situation, it is a destructive phenomenon. As a recourse in moments of confusion and disorientation, projective identification fills the bill for many scapegoaters. Seeing in themselves qualities that they are not proud of, they attempt to ascribe these qualities to their own children, who in their fantasies become responsible for the parents' own problems.

The term projective identification, originally used by Melanie Klein (1946) to describe some types of intrapsychic and interpersonal processes, denotes an individual's projection of undesired or sometimes even highly desirable traits from the self onto others. A clearer view of the process of projective identification emerges from Thomas Ogden's (1979) description of its four phases: (1) the projector wishes to shift or entertains the fantasy of shifting highly desirable or undesirable aspects of self onto another person; (2) the projector transforms or induces in the projectee feelings that will correspond to the desires or fantasies of the projector; (3) the projectee, particularly one who is vulnerable, accepts and "processes" the projection; (4) the projector begins to reaccept or internalize the "processed" projection of the projectee.

This formulation shows that projective identification is not just a transpersonal defense mechanism, but it can be understood as a process that characterizes a number of nonpathological interpersonal interactions. For instance, think of a father who is a high achiever but never fulfilled his dream of becoming a heart surgeon. If he projects this desire onto his son at an early age, the child (the projectee) may accept that image and see the dream as his own.

Projective identification has been variously interpreted. Originally, Melanie Klein viewed projective identification as a process of defense or control initiated by the child and directed at one of his or her parents. In most psychoanalytically oriented schools, however, family therapists regard parents as the initiators of transpersonal processes that could be used for purposes of defense or control. From the psychoanalytic point of view, parents are the ones who tend to project their "narcissistic desires onto their children" (Richter, 1960; 1963), somehow delegating or forcing these children to fulfill their needs in various ways.

In view of the apparent diversity of opinion, a question arises concerning the relative power and dependency of the transactional partners in the projective processes. In discussing dependency between partners who are relatively similar in status, Wynne and associates (1958) speak of "trading dissociations," meaning that there is a form of reciprocity through delegation or collusions. If delegation is in the service of parental self-observation, it can be explained that delegates must incorporate into their personality the denied or rejected aspects of the parents' personalities so that the parents can have their rejected aspects at a safe but observable distance (Simon, Stierlin, & Wynne, 1985). The term collusion refers to a secret agreement between two or more persons for deceitful or fraudulent purposes (American Heritage Dictionary, 1982). If the partners are unequal in power, the weaker, dependent partner may adopt the stronger or older person's reality (Stierlin, 1959). For example, 10-year-old Adrian picked up on his father's desires for easy money and therefore became involved in a number of shoplifting incidents, which his family overlooked. Adrian was reciprocal to his father in terms of delegation and collusion.

Attendant Conditions

Bowen (1978) has employed the term family projection process in a unique way that only partially overlaps the concept of projective identification. Bowen understands the projective identification process as the basic process by which parents project problems onto their children. The effects of these problems on the children could range all the way from very mild symptoms to the severest forms of schizophrenia and autism. Looking at it in a traditional sense, the basic process involves an emotional system that is more focused on the children than on the parents. A wife who is sensitive to her husband's concerns supports his emotional involvement and desire to have their children excel academically. At times this may make the children overly anxious.

The family projection system is a universal phenomenon in that it occurs in all families to some extent. It alleviates the anxiety of undifferentiation in the present generation at the expense of the following generation. And it is often true that the system functions better at the expense of one of its members. Thus through the family projection process the level of parental differentiation is passed on to the children. The child becomes the burden or symptom bearer of the family (Bowen, 1978).

Grotstein (1985) indicates that projective identification takes place during a child's formative years. His profoundly perceptive description of the basic mechanism involves the following: (1) along with splitting, the process entails omnipotent denial, idealization, and introjection as defenses against persecutory anxiety; (2) projective identification and splitting go hand in hand. When a child has to behave in ways that are often not comfortable, this can mark the beginning of the splitting-off process, where the child splits and projective identification acts as an adjunct to splitting, assigning a split-off percept of self to a container for postponement or for eradication. So it was in the case of Kate, who at the age of five had to file her father's nails and then satisfy him sexually. As a young adult in her early twenties, Kate recalled the filing of his nails. Then she said, glancing up at me, "Then someone else took over. It was not me."

Grotstein asserts that projective identification and projection are identical and interchangeable terms. He says that the degree of splitting that attends the projection determines the degree to which it relies on disidentification of the self or reidentification of the self in the object, whether the object is intrapsychic or interpersonal. However, Wolheim (1969) distinguishes between projection and projective identification on content and aim. With respect to content, mental qualities are *projected* and internal objects are projectively identified. With reference to the aim, projection involves a wish to remain in contact with the thoughts or ideas, located in the external object, for reassurance; in contrast, projective identification entails the wish to be rid of the thought and the internal object, and thus tends toward a state of thoughtlessness. Grotstein, conceding that this distinction could be technically correct, makes the practical point that it is hard to recognize differences like those while working in a clinical situation. Ogden (1978, 1979), Meissner (1980), and Ornston (1978) make a distinction that seems relevant to our understanding of these concepts. They see projection as an intrapsychic mechanism and projective identification as a transactional or bipersonal mechanism.

There can be no projective identification in a vacuum.

The translocation of self or aspects of self into an object always presupposes a preconception of an object that is a container. Location of an object by means of scanning, foraging, or exploration reveals a primitive mechanism of normal thinking.

Views of Projective Identification

All projective identifications imply two states of anxiety, one that precedes and one that follows the projection. The original anxiety is a consequence of the experience of separation and precipitates the projective identification, which in turn gives rise to a second state of anxiety.

A projective identification can be neurotic or psychotic in character. Neurotic projective identification is experienced as an extension into an object that has previously been believed to be separate. Psychotic projective identification is characterized by a withdrawal of the surviving self from this object and from the ego boundaries that previously defined the self. The object and ego boundaries usually become confused with each other, transforming the bizarre object into an amalgam of delusion and hallucinations.

Interpersonal projective identification should be distinguished from intrapsychic projective identification, although the two may overlap.

Grotstein (1985) describes splitting as an agent of the principle of differentiation, and projective identification as the agent of the principle of generalization. This pair of forces constitutes the lowest common denominator of all defense mechanisms, as well as driving the perceptions and thought processes through varying degrees of displacement and secondary recombination. In the end,

repression, denial, isolation, intellectualization, and identification with the aggressor are all considered to be
combinations of splitting and projective identification. Just
as thinking and perception involve anticipation, selection,
and reorganization of the gestalt or perception for mental
storage, it is believed that splitting and projective identification are fundamentally involved in these processes of
anticipation, selection, and reorganization. Splitting corresponds to differentiation and projective identification
corresponds to externalization as it anticipates perception.

Like splitting, projective identification can be seen in
terms of object relationships. Meltzer (1967) describes the
sequence of the infant's projections into and from different
parts of its body—for instance, the oral, anal, and genital
zones—which the infant perceives in relation to itself and
its parent. This process creates a confusion of boundaries
between the zones of its body and those of the parent's
body.

It can be said that defensive projective identification
involves the splitting off and evacuation of objects of mind,
that is, feelings and thoughts and the translocations of "I"
or a portion of "I" that is the subject of the mind into a
transforming identification with an object. In psychosis
the mind itself is evacuated and the "I" either disappears
altogether or delusionally *becomes* the object, not merely
something identified with it. This person "I" may disclaim
or even attempt to murder the impostor who currently
misrepresents him or her.

Grotstein refers to another kind of psychotic projective
identification in the experience of *telekinesis*. The psychotic
may identify projectively with a split-off self—that is, a
disembodied twin self that is free to move about anywhere
it likes, including leaving the body in what amounts to

self-abandonment. This application concludes Grotstein's comprehensive description of projective identification.

In therapy 42-year-old Thalia complained that the main problem was her 20-year-old daughter, Patti, who would not come into therapy with her. Thalia wanted me to call Patti, but after an hour of discussion she realized that she should take responsibility for bringing her daughter in. She described Patti as incorrigible, complaining that she was promiscuous and spent all her money on clothes, jewelry, and entertainment.

When Patti at last came for therapy, I was amazed at the resemblance between mother and daughter. They were even similarly dressed in casual but stylish fashion, with elaborate makeup and hairdos. The mother complained that the daughter did not work, but always had a good time. Further discussion revealed that Thalia supplied Patti with a free apartment, a truck and the gas to run it, and the pocket money to live her life. I wondered where was the need for the daughter to work when she was given no incentives.

As the case unfolded, it became clear that the mother was projecting her identification and needs into this daughter. As a single parent, she constantly brought up the topic of her daughter's promiscuity, which the daughter halfheartedly denied. Eventually, we decided that we needed to meet with Patti's boyfriend, whom Thalia considered to be a bad influence on Patti. On the day the three came to see me, I was once again startled to see the mother dressed in the style of her daughter. Thalia was also openly flirtatious with Patti's boyfriend, so much so that Patti became uneasy. After a short while, I asked the boyfriend to leave. When he had gone, Patti started to fight angrily with Thalia, ridiculing her and her behavior. At that, Thalia gave me a triumphant look and proclaimed, "Now you see— that just proves what I'm telling you: she's incorrigible." Thalia might not have looked so triumphant if she could have seen how faithfully Patti reflected Thalia's own qualities and characteristics.

Later on in therapy, Thalia revealed that she had always wanted to have a life of her own, with everything provided for her by her parents, but this had never happened. What's more, she admitted, giggling uncontrollably, she wished she had had a number of boyfriends and lovers just as her daughter did.

In this case, some degree of projective identification had taken place. However, in her conscious mind, the mother saw all this behavior as emitting purely from the daughter and failed to recognize her role in the situation.

DISIDENTIFICATION

Rejecting the Role of the Scapegoat

When a person identifies with someone else to the point of hurting himself or herself and realizes that this condition is unhealthy for self-development, disidentification follows. A person who has participated in the projective identification process for a long time and who has been hurt by it may seek a way out of it if survival is at stake— even while seeing himself or herself as the bearer of the family's problems. Therapy, especially long-term therapy, can point the way. Occasionally people who have unquestionably taken on responsibility for most of the family problems for most of their lives suddenly or gradually, with or without therapy, come to a realization that they have been the burden bearers for the entire family, and they no longer wish to play the role.

Irene, for example, was a 30-year-old family scapegoat who had not yet separated herself from her family of origin. With sudden insight, she said in therapy that she was the family's "safe container" for bearing their problems and painful experiences.

Irene learned to acknowledge the unfairness of her parents' rejection. She no longer showed a desire to rush to the defense of her parents. Describing herself and her situation, she said that she was very unfairly dumped on, and as she spoke she grew very angry: "I am not going to take all the blame in the family," she declared. "This was also their doing." When clients start learning to dissociate themselves from the family situation, this is the beginning of disidentification with all the problems of the family. Usually this clear perception of the situation is preceded by a period of rage and blame in which the scapegoated person expresses the feeling of having been used. The person's awareness of his or her role in the family comes out either verbally or in action.

Many scapegoated persons must physically separate themselves from the family. After this necessary estrangement, they attempt to consolidate the new, good-enough self or individual ego. Later they may even come to accept the family members who have hurt them, though at first they were viewed as the rejecting ones. They may try to see those family members themselves as victims struggling unaided against strong negative forces. Forgiveness is a potent healer, for the wronged as well as the wrongdoer. The former scapegoat comes to see parents as people with problems like everyone else—no longer omnipotent, but just human, the victims of their own misfortunes.

Beyond Rage and Blame

Gloria, a woman in her early thirties, was the youngest of 13 children. Her father was very strict with the children, requiring every one of them to be home by 6:00 P.M. He was rude and verbally abusive to his other children, but it was Gloria who bore the brunt of his anger. In her early years he would beat her whenever she accidentally wet her bed. Gloria learned to read her father's moods. She knew by the way he drove the car into the garage whether he would beat her or not. She also gauged his temper by his slamming of the front door as he entered the house. At times she would be so afraid that she would hide when she heard him come home; this behavior would infuriate him, and he would beat her anyway.

All her pent-up anger changed her into a terror at school. She defied her teachers, damaged school property, shrugged off the principal's disciplinary measures, and attracted a wild crowd of trouble-prone youngsters.

By the time Gloria was 14, her father had made a habit of issuing daily warnings to her and her sisters. He would remind them every day that they were going out as single women and that when they returned home, he better not see any changes in their behaviors or bodies. If he did, he added, he would kill them right there in the house. This self-righteousness angered Gloria, who was aware that her father had been seeing other women though he was married. Defiantly, Gloria started to run around with boys behind his back. When she was 16, he died of a heart attack. Gloria then became extremely promiscuous and went out with any man for the asking. One-night stands became a way of life for her. However, during the past year she had become celibate, realizing that she had been hurting herself by her behavior. Besides counseling, her fear of AIDS also played a role in bringing about change in her behavior.

One day when Gloria had been in therapy for a few months, she remarked that her father had died when he received news of his mother's death in another town. It was strange because he died of a heart attack the same day, a few hours after he heard the dreadful news of his mother's death. Moved by her new insight, she said that she should forgive him for his behavior and not be so uptight about him anymore; he was a very troubled man, she said, whom nobody liked—not even her mother who constantly complained about him. The only person who really cared about him and whom he trusted was his mother, and her death brought about his. She added, "Poor man. Today, I feel sorry for him. He was a very lonely, sick man." As an afterthought, she added that he had not known any better than to do as he did, having been physically abused by his father. For Gloria, this awareness marked the beginning of her own healing. Seeing her father as a weak, unhappy person, not as a strong, tyrannical punisher, helped her come to terms with her feelings about him.

In many cases, disidentification cannot take place before the client has gone through a retributive stage, feeling that if he or she has had to suffer, others should do the same. In the beginning of therapy, therefore, the client may be vindictive and enviously destructive, given to angry outbursts and temper tantrums. The client feels that the problem is not his or hers alone but that other family members should share the burden. If these other members are participating in therapy, they very well may.

Somehow the client seems to find it easier to forgive the scapegoaters when those individuals are also present in the treatment process. The desire for revenge is commonly expressed in statements during therapy such as: "I am tired of playing their game"; "I am feeling worthless because of them"; and "I want them to suffer for a change." Therapists not only have to be patient with such statements, but also should manifest full acceptance of their import. For this is the beginning of disidentification from the accuser and victim aspects of the scapegoated self. It is also the beginning of the conscious, individual assertion that will carry the scapegoated person toward wellness. But before the scapegoated person can take on questions of identity, the person will have to acknowledge his or her own anguish and anger, examine them, and learn to go beyond the symptoms of guilt-bearing and martyred self-rejection that are the main components of the negatively inflated identity. Jung (1953–1979) puts it this way:

> No matter how much parents and grandparents may have sinned against the child, the man who is really adult will accept sins as his own conditions which have to be reckoned with. Only a fool is interested in other people's guilt, since he cannot alter it. The wise man learns only from his own guilt. He will ask himself: "Who am I that all this should happen to me?" To find the answer to this fateful question he will look into his own heart (p. 152).

The scapegoated person has to learn and relearn the art of communicating with his or her own family of origin. Then come questions like "Why me?" and "What is my part in this whole family scenario?" Before going out and dealing with others, the person needs to deal with his or her own pains and claim the power in the family to act assertively and aggressively within the collective of his or her needs. An understanding of the destructive entitlement and family dynamics in the family of origin helps the client move toward working at his or her own issues. It is only after this, that the person can function in terms of individual vocation and life choices. Attempts at being nonassertive with family members who have scapegoated a person does not foster disidentification from the scapegoated feelings that this person experiences. Thus, understanding family patterns and developing assertiveness is a long, rough, bumpy road, and working with these types of clients takes time as they have to understand and accept their situation reasonably well.

DEVELOPING A SENSE OF IDENTITY

Scapegoated people have been overwhelmed with negatives for so long that living with positives requires a major adjustment. The negative self-concept is extremely difficult to replace with the self-image of a fairly well-adjusted person.

Satir (1972) pointed out that people value themselves according to the value that close family members place on them. Self-esteem and a sense of identity are regulated by mechanisms of mutual appreciation and depreciation. Normally the standards for evaluating one's own worth are developed in the family of origin and are later transferred to the other relationships that one develops. But the severely scapegoated person is incapable of developing a stable sense of self-esteem because of the internal relationships and patterns of communication that have developed in the family of origin, which encourage a sense of worthlessness in the person. However, the family alone is not responsible for an individual's self-esteem. Other factors such as job success and social acceptance are important contributors to the development and maintenance of self-respect. An individual's autonomy depends upon the degree to which he or she is able to maintain a sense of self-esteem in the absence of external validation.

However, because of the inadequate differentiation (fusion) between self and object, exhibiting itself in a tendency toward fusion with the object and an inability to form a constructive relationship to the object; it can be said that the process of progressive differentiation between self and object goes hand in hand with the process of relatedness. Hopefully, this process happens in therapy if it is not already present.

As discussed earlier, the concept of the real self refers to the normal, healthy intrapsychic self, its object relations, and their related affects. The cornerstone of a person's real self is the sense of self-entitlement where the person feels entitled to mastery and to whatever this commitment requires. This concept includes the person's capacities for self-activation, assertion, and commitment. But in the scapegoated person there is a split between the real self and the false, defensive self. The false, defensive self is not based on reality but is there to defend the person against painful affect at the cost of reality. For instance, a client who has poor self-esteem will not have supportive self-assertion. This person cannot acknowledge self-worth, experience self-activation and mastery, and feel self-entitlement, soothe intense affects, identify the self's unique individuated wishes and activate them into reality, or make and pursue a commitment (Masterson, 1985). Because of these negative factors the person resorts to avoidance, passivity, denial, and fantasy which further contribute to the lack of self-esteem.

Some persons whose self-esteem is low become anxious and depressed as they begin to assert themselves; immediately, then, they cut off all feeling and again give up the self-assertion. One young woman, Mindy, described her mother's use of complaints to manipulate her; in order to satisfy her mother's needs, Mindy becomes her mother's idea of a "good, nice girl" which takes over her real self.

In these people there is an avoidance of spontaneous expression of the real self with a self-image of feeling good. The illusory qualities of the defensive self is shown by its content and motives and by the denial and devaluation of reality they require (Masterson, 1985): thus, the content revolves around the person's worthlessness and unwantedness.

The whole purpose of the therapeutic work with these clients is to help them achieve the therapeutic alliance: a real object relationship is developed, with the client's wellness as the goal. At the commencement of therapy the therapist makes clear to the client this understanding of the reality of the relationship.

To enable clients to work through their emotions, the therapist should be as neutral as possible. The therapist should provide enormous amounts of positive support, which is a powerful therapeutic aid that emphasizes the clients' potentials and creates a favorable climate for their therapeutic work. The value of this support to scapegoated people cannot be overstated: for the first time in their lives, they are perceived, acknowledged, and responded to in terms of their own emotional needs and best interests. By monitoring what clients can handle and proceeding with great care, the therapist can provide their clients with the greatest support. The interview becomes a vehicle for the client's expression and for discharging of painful emotions, and a context in which to review critical efforts to solve adaptive problems and to rehearse new adaptive solutions.

One of the most important matters that clients have to feel responsible for is their own commitment to treatment. Often, clients are asked to think through issues, write about their problems, and draw pictures of their family and feelings with the sole purpose of moving them toward caring and feeling responsible for their own well-being.

To see the kind of help these clients need in developing their own self-identity, consider Mahler, Pine, and Bergman's (1975) study of normal separation and individuation as it occurs with children. They describe the toddler's self-assertive explorations of the environment, followed by a return to the mother to "ask" nonverbally for support. When the mother provides this support, it renews the child's attempts at self-assertive exploration of the environment. Mahler and her coworkers call this effect "refueling." Refueling encompasses two issues: (1) to provide the child or an adult client with the required feeling of closeness and acceptance; and (2) to provide emotional acknowledgment and support for the child's unfolding real self as seen in his or her self-assertive explorations. This process, all the more critical because it is belated, is what the therapist must accomplish metaphorically in order to help the client outgrow infantile dependencies and learn to satisfy his or her own needs.

With persistent efforts a therapist can help unhook a scapegoated client and foster self-esteem also through such intervention strategies as enactment, and marking boundaries. Enactment is a technique where the therapist asks the family to actually do what they are describing to the therapist. The therapist attempts to construct an interpersonal scenario in the session in which dysfunctional transactions among family members are played out. In some of the cases I handled the family members were not present; however, I used empty chairs to indicate to the client the presence of these family members and asked the client to best represent how they would react to each other.

The therapist can also actualize transactional patterns by refusing to respond even when addressed directly, which forces the family members (or the client and chairs representing family members) to show what they actually *do* when left to their own resources. In this situation, the therapist is in a position to observe the family members' verbal and nonverbal ways of signaling to each other and to monitor the range of tolerable transactions. Therefore, the therapist can work with the flexibility of the family's transactions in search of solutions and also has the possibility of coping with family situations in different ways which all help in building up clients' confidence and self-esteem.

Therapy also includes defining and clarifying relationships between different members by marking boundaries and helping clients to take the "I" position in their communications. In addition, therapy involves helping clients understand the relational family patterns which include understanding family loyalty and its implications for fairness in family dynamics; the role of responsibility in working out family issues; and the place of entitlement in their lives, be it constructive or destructive entitlement, and its effects on the behaviors of family members. The essence of therapy lies in the enhancement of the quality of clients' lives.

THE THERAPEUTIC PROCESS

Throughout their lives scapegoated persons suffer from feelings of emotional abandonment and anger. With interventions from a supportive therapist the client starts to refuel the real self. In time, the client will pursue new interests with persistence and continuity and, equally important, a new sense of spontaneity, entitlement, and vigor. In the beginning, however, the client relies heavily on the defensive self and avoids real self-activation, denying the price he or she pays in reality for that avoidance. For instance, from childhood through adolescence Dawn had been sexually abused by her father. At 20 years of age, she felt defensive about revealing this information to her family, particularly to her mother, and said, "It's all right. I don't want to hurt them. I'm grown up now and I don't even want to hurt my father. Anyway, he's in enough trouble as it is." Through therapy the client realizes that there are two important activities he or she can work at constantly: (1) expressing one's own unique real self; and (2) turning a passive mode into an active, self-assertive one.

The therapist must find the communicative patterns best suited to the particular needs of client. For example, the therapist must remember, despite temptation and the sense of urgency of the client's situation, not to direct, force, seduce, or intimidate the client into activating the real self. That awakening has to come from within the client—and in the client's own time. Sometimes the client's steps toward the goal seem maddeningly small. The therapist's strategy then is to show the client that a triumph shared is doubled, whereas a defeat shared is halved.

Reparenting is also used as a method in therapy for working through the client's deprived infantile emotional needs. Through transference the client sees the therapist in the role of approving parent who acknowledges the client's emerging self and aids the client to deal with his or her childhood deprivations.

Clients sometimes deliberately fail in their undertakings because they do not know how to experience success, which would align them with their real selves. Having experienced themselves as small and insignificant, they feel bad about their positive accomplishments. They may also find that the thought of being their real selves, though exhilarating, makes them anxious. One client said, "I constantly subject my own ideas to whatever objections or criticism I raise and then give up. I am afraid to run my own life" (Masterson, 1985, p. 67).

These people have experienced so much guilt that when blamed by others they become defensive. Their suffering is to them a symptom of their own failures and proof of their own wrongdoing, which therefore adds to the burden of guilt they carry. However, as scapegoated clients become more comfortable with themselves, they are less likely to avoid risks, and slowly but definitely they are ready to take on life with all its uncertainty.

In love and other close personal relationships, basic incompatibilities exist side by side; the need for togetherness and the need for distance inevitably occur, to varying degrees and at various times. The scapegoated person does not know to make the distinction, but with help and understanding the person can reach a point of discrimination.

Through inner guidance, caring acceptance, and objectivity, the therapist helps to negate and process the negative parental complexes that need to be transformed. This work slowly enables the client's hidden, true self to emerge. This self learns to discover seeing and being seen objectively.

The healing process is a difficult one: it is based on the skills of the therapist and the unfolding of the therapeutic process. For instance, 37-year-old Priscilla is the victim of sexual abuse and has also abused her own children. Dealing with this severely scapegoated woman involved work with her family, her peers, and her children's school system. It is fairly common, if available, to utilize all the systems in that person's life to help her or him toward wellness. Priscilla has now been in the healing process for over a year. Therapeutic work with her has been long, arduous, rewarding, and frustrating.

In the healing process, through the phase of nurturance, the scapegoated person finds the ability to endure frustration, to assert, and to accept dependency and independence. One client put it to his therapist this way:

> I can feel a home. Rootedness on earth. I get a sense of goodness and strength and passionate intensity as connected to me, so I am not just bad and guilty. I can see myself alive and whole because you see me that way—because you see all of me, not just ugly fragments (Perera, 1985, p. 85).

5

Therapy with Three Scapegoated Clients

GEORGE AND FAMILY: HEALING THE SCAPEGOAT

A Disturbed Adolescent

Fourteen-year-old George came from a family of six children. He was the youngest child and had been labeled as disturbed. He was well known for roughhousing with other children and for getting into trouble. However, he considered himself very bright and would do anything to prove this to anyone. I suspected his sophisticated vocabulary was the result of his constant exposure to the therapist's world.

I met with George a few times without having any real communication. He began to test me by constantly and persistently asking me for things I could not give him, or by asking for permission to get away from the special education school he had to attend.

The Incident

George fascinated me. The first time I met him I could not see his face except for his eyes; he covered himself with his jacket hood by zipping it up to his nose and covering his face up to his forehead. He almost always had his face covered at least up to his mouth. However, after the third session at my insistence he removed the jacket. What I saw was gruesome. George had a deep scar around his lips which made his mouth extremely unsightly. With smoldering pain, and at times with amusement—which almost felt like tears to me—George playfully yet sadly started to relate the incident that led to his facial scars. Remorsefully, he remembered how he had been robbed of his looks.

When he was five years of age, his parents had had a formidable argument. At that time, George felt thirsty and wanted to drink some milk from a carton that his mother had placed near the stove. His mother, Vera, typically told him not to touch it as it was not yet time for his drink, whereas his father, Douglas, ventilating all his anger against his wife in a no-win situation, vehemently cajoled George to get the milk and drink it. Although his father appeared to be a peripheral figure in the family when the tension between his parents became unbearable, George was always caught in the middle of it and usually ended up being beaten by Douglas, or more often, by Vera. This was one of those days. Vera bellowed that George should not touch the milk. Caught between the two of them, it became clear that he had to obey his father whose temper he feared most. When George picked up the carton of milk, his mother, in a fit of anger and unrelenting fury, pushed George's face into the burning stove. No medical treatments truly helped in removing the burn and he was left with a permanent huge shiny scar on his face around his lips. As mentioned previously, George saw this scar (his burnt lips) as being the main cause of all his problems. Thus, he was caught in his own negative body image and did not blame his mother.

Based on the boundless available information, it was clear that George had been the designated family scapegoat from the time he was born. His mother did not like him because he was darker than the rest of her children and she considered him ugly. He had very clear heavy features which she did not like. Often she would keep him away from her relatives and friends, saying that he was away doing something; in reality, he might have been sitting in his bedroom, which he was usually ordered to do.

At a young age, George became a formidable tease which revealed both the accuser and victim aspects of his personality; he learned to ridicule and laugh at his parents when they asked him to do anything, thus provoking severe punishment. At the same time, he was never sure whom he should obey as he was afraid of the harrowing tempers of both parents. Compounding these emotional burdens, there was a constant lack of money in the household. Douglas would come home angry and drunk, and Vera would start to scream and yell at him about the financial situation. His maternal grandmother, Elsie May, also lived with them and criticized the son-in-law to her daughter and the grandchildren.

George grew up in a home where there were many inconsistencies: George was confused about what was expected of him and what he could do or could not do. He experienced contradictory emotions like love and hate, and this led him to being indecisive about his feelings and also to shift rapidly emotional attitudes toward the people in his life. Elsie May had a formidable temper and all kinds of ravages were inflicted on people who crossed her path. However, George mentioned that he loved her very much because she was kinder to him than to any other adult in the family. But George at a young age learned to fear for his safety when his parents and grandmother got into a fight.

After several sessions, George, with agitation, talked about an incident that loomed ominously over his head for a number of years, which left a permanent scar on him. He could not really recall why, but his mother and father got into another one of their violent arguments. In a fit of rage, Douglas started to beat Vera. Elsie May, who was sitting in the kitchen, rushed to her daughter's rescue and started to beat on and curse Douglas. In a fit of temper, Douglas took the butcher knife and stabbed his mother-in-law again and again until she fell to the kitchen floor, making it red, bloody, and messy. Petrified George witnessed the whole scene. Later he remembered that the police came and took his father away as his grandmother lay dying of the stab wounds. He remembered the putrid odors in the room long after this incident happened. George was in deep despair as he was very fond of his grandmother. He considered her to be the most affectionate person in their home.

Acting-out Behaviors

For a long time George had nightmares about this incident. He was too afraid to trust or to confide in anyone. He walked around like a phantom at home, panicked that if he did anything wrong his mother might kill him. Thus, school became a relief. George could very easily get away with any kind of behavior, and he loved the relative freedom and the lack of venomous tension. However, his worst behavior started to appear when he turned 10. George would provoke both teachers and students to a point of total exasperation. All he cared about was that he could behave anyway he liked, and yet he would not be punished as severely at school as he would be at home.

However, when George was 11, his problems came to the forefront when his frolic turned to aggressive and abusive behavior. He got into fights with his classmates and beat them up, blue and black, but would not take responsibility for it. When such an incident happened right within the classroom, he was suspended from school. Eventually he ended up in a residential treatment setting. He had lived in this setting for three years when I met him. At this time George's father was in jail and would not be eligible for parole for another six years. His mother saw George as the institution's responsibility and started to distance herself from George and the agency.

As George's behavior continued to deteriorate, he got into trouble with his teacher by constantly playing tricks on her. One incident brought to my notice was that he had choked a secretary on the way to my office. In panic, she came running to me holding her throat; George followed her, saying that he was only "playing." I realized that he was rough and had to bind him strictly to reality while he attempted to wiggle out of the situation. When I asked him to apologize, George complained that the secretary was a "sissy" and that he was only having fun with her. Eventually he apologized when he realized he had left marks on her neck.

Since George came from an abusive background, he often did things that were unacceptable to others but which he did not view seriously until his attention was forcefully brought to the matter. From that time on, George's behavior in the office building was restricted to seeing me—when I went and fetched him from the front door. Instead of being unhappy, he was excited that I would walk to the front door and walk him back to my office. He saw this as a privilege, and I believe it satisfied his attention-seeking needs.

As mentioned in Chapter 4, George loved humor and I used it frequently in therapy with him. Using jokes and talking about comics that he enjoyed helped him relax and led the way to more intensive therapy work with him. He also learned to use his humor constructively. Constantly, reality was brought to him strictly in terms of what was acceptable as normal teenage behavior. Though George would giggle, he learned very quickly that I meant what I said. Oftentimes, he would ask me if he was the worst kid I was working with. I responded by saying that every child in the setting had some problem, and though George had his own problems, he was still a special person. My caring attitude had a number of effects on George. The more concern I showed him, the better his behavior got. Thus, a warm, safe therapeutic atmosphere had been created for him.

Change in Behavior

George started to perform well in school and requested guitar lessons. I made arrangements for the lessons, provided that he was responsible and paid a few dollars from his pocket money. As George learned to contain his emotions appropriately, he was allowed more privileges at his residential cottage. We also made arrangements to take him to a plastic surgeon so that his scars around his lips could be treated. The resident psychiatrist was just as amazed as I was at George's self-control. I personally felt that George was responding to me as an adult who cared about him but who could also set clear limits on what was acceptable or not acceptable in his behavior.

I recall that in one of my first therapy sessions with him, George was totally out of control. He would run in and out of my office, bang my office door, and scream at the secretary (who was frightened of him) who sat at her desk at the end of the hallway. This reflected, in many ways, his chaotic home atmosphere. When I asked him what he was gaining by this behavior, he responded cleverly, half-amused, half-serious, with comical alacrity that adolescents like himself were supposed to misbehave. Sternly, I warned him I would not accept any behavior that was painful or hurtful to others. As time passed, it seemed that George had learned to control his behavior more and more.

George's most ardent wish was to meet one of his older brothers who was a member of a singing group. His desire to play the guitar was based on the fact that he admired and wanted to be like his older brother Peter. Realizing that Peter would be a good role model, we called and corresponded with his brother, who wrote back to him sporadically.

Transference

George had extremely positive feelings toward me and I was aware of it. The word "transference" has come to be used rather loosely and sometimes inappropriately for all the feelings the client has for the therapist. One of the first feelings I experienced with George was distrust. This was natural, of course, though it can be said that this relationship had "transference aspects" in the sense that the patient's trust had been betrayed in the past. In any case, it is often important to bring such feelings to the surface and to work with them. The mere fact that the therapist is willing to accept that he or she is not necessarily trusted in itself may engender trust (Malan, 1979).

Off and on, George had brought up the topic of his mother and how he would love to visit her. I agreed to go with him and visit his mother who lived 50 miles away. George smiled at me and said that I probably would do anything for him. In return, I smiled. I realized the intensity of his feelings for me and the incontrovertible evidence that these feelings were transferred from someone in his past. As I saw it, the someone could have been his grandmother or sister. However, I felt a considerable degree of security and self-knowledge to face such transference and to handle it appropriately. For me, it constituted an important therapeutic tool, making it possible to work through some feelings that had long been buried. George's session ended and he left my office. However, that evening he came back at around 5:00 P.M. and told me he had something important he needed to ask. Fourteen-year-old George stared at me and asked if I would untie and loosen my long hair and go out with him for dinner that evening. I must admit that I was taken aback by this sexual approach. I quickly recovered my composure, and it became clear that erotic feelings are only one example of a whole range of intense feelings that a client may develop for a therapist. These feelings can be worked through, provided they are confined to verbal expressions and their origins in the past and present are explored.

Though transference was originally seen as a hindrance to therapy and a necessary evil, it is now regarded as an important means of understanding and analyzing the client, since past conflicts are revived and arise in the here-and-now in front of the therapist's eyes (Malan, 1979). However, more out of surprise than anything else, I immediately replied by asking George whether he needed to know anything about sex and by offering to share a book on human anatomy with him. He, in turn, was taken aback: he quickly refused my offer and hurriedly left my office. This was the first and last time George ever made such comments to me, but I was very aware that there were transferred feelings.

In retrospect, I realized that George had constantly compared me to his older sister, Shirley. He saw me as his sister, a giving, caring, and trustworthy person. To be sexually attracted to me could be viewed as a normal reaction to an attractive woman. However, in spite of my self-awareness, I became uncomfortable at his remarks. My behavior might have had the effect of shutting off any further discussion of his feelings toward me or of his own sexuality. After this incident and my reflections on it, I progressively used his positive feelings for me to help toward his own growth.

George often mentioned that he loved his mother, though it appeared that after the grandmother's death his sister Shirley was his chief caretaker. Every child should have love for his parent, he explained, adding defensively that whatever a mother does to a child is all right as she is the person responsible for his or her birth and entrance into this world. I wondered from whom and why George had learned to share such thoughts. I questioned whether this kind of reasoning would make it easier for him to accept his mother (who had permanently disfigured his face). As is the case in similar situations, this scapegoated adolescent's desire to meet and please her was very intense.

The Home Visit

After a lengthy correspondence we paid a home visit. Vera, George's mother, lived in a old-fashioned brick house. She was a good-looking, fair-skinned African-American with startling brown eyes. My heart sank as I realized that George certainly had not inherited any of her good looks, a fact which had been held against him. As we entered the house, Vera talked to me and looked at her son but made no effort to hug him although she had not seen him in a couple of years. As a matter of fact, she asked George how he was doing, as if he were attending a private school, and then dismissed the subject. All her children had left home permanently except the youngest daughter, Rowena, who was older than George. A couple of the children lived with their older sister, Shirley, who was married and lived a few minutes from the mother. Rowena was an attractive pregnant teenager with her mother's good looks. She glanced toward her brother, gave him a pleasant smile, and went about the chores as requested by the mother. Once in a while, she would turn around and stare at her mother resentfully.

Vera took us to the kitchen, but George got up and wandered around the house. Calling out to George, she offered us milk to drink. George did not want any. I watched her with ominous admiration as she moved to the refrigerator, pulled out a carton of milk, drank directly from the carton, and then put the carton back. Throughout my session with her, she walked to the refrigerator and drank more milk. It appeared to me that she was an empty container, trying desperately to fill herself, but perhaps she could never fill up. Vera spoke well of all her children, particularly Peter, her son who was a musical band leader. She looked at George and sighed as if the past seeds of destructive tendencies toward him were still there.

When I tried to find out if she had any plans for George's future, her face became distraught with anger and pain. The scapegoater in her came out. In an anguished voice, she said that only after George was born there had been trouble in her marriage and now her husband was in prison. She did not give me details of her mother's death. Vera appeared to be an infantile person who somehow in the back of her mind saw George as being responsible for all her marital problems. I attempted to communicate in a simple overt manner. Firmly suppressing the doubts I had about her story, I tried to talk to Vera about George's improvements, including his guitar lessons and his school performance. She was stoically silent.

George was not able to talk to his mother beyond polite surface topics. The appearance she presented was that of a person who had been hurt and offended by this child George. In reality, George's behavior to a large extent was the result of a chaotic, severely emotionally distressed family situation. Since I had sincerely hoped that the mother and George could get back together, I invited her for the Mothers' meetings that took place in the residential setting, promising her train or bus fare both ways. She agitatedly declined the offer. The clear message she was giving me was that she did not wish George to come back home. Though I suspected that there were issues between her and the daughter living at home, she seemed focused on seeing George as the problem. This was a painful experience for me as I saw a mother continually ostracize and reject her son for her own problems. I was not sure how much information George absorbed because he became very quiet, quite unlike his behavior at the agency.

After Vera subtly made her point that she was not ready for George, she kept walking to the refrigerator to drink milk. George went to see his old bedroom, and then I decided that it was time to leave. Though obviously resentful of her mother, Rowena sequaciously followed Vera's behavior and kept away from George.

As we were leaving, my heart went out to George, who pretended that it did not matter. The mother put her head out the open window and commented to George that he could come to live with her when he had a job.

George and I walked brusquely to the subway station and I rattled my brain about how I would deal with this situation in our therapy sessions. I wondered if more harm had been done by this home visit. I was filled with remorse for George. Both of us were rather quiet on the way back to the residential setting. George, by way of explanation, told me that his mother had always been that way, that she was not good at hugging, but he knew she loved him as she had asked him to return home when he had a job. I had other thoughts about this but did not share them.

After we returned to the treatment center, George's behavior, as expected, deteriorated. He got into trouble with his teacher and did everything possible in a negative way to get my attention. He threw temper tantrums, had fist fights with other children, and viewed me with surprise when I did not use his behavior to reject him (as he expected).

Thinking of George's mother, I realized that Vera would take him back if he was a financial provider for her, but at the same time, her coldness and accusing looks told me a different story: George would continue to be scapegoated. Unfortunately, she was not ready for therapy.

Future Plans

We made plans to send George to a group home for independent living when he turns 16. I continued to encourage diligently the relationship that was beginning to develop between George and his brother, Peter. They learned to talk to and enjoy each other on the phone. Eventually, Peter visited George and I believe this development of a relationship with a brother whom he really admired was one of the best gifts he could have received.

There were a number of unfinished and unresolved issues in George's life, one of the biggest gaps being that he had no contact with his father since the age of five. However, his most serious issue was the relationship with his mother that did not progress. This caused him constant anguish, and often he attempted to defend his mother's behavior, another characteristic of the scapegoated person. With a tremendous amount of work between us, George attempted to understand and accept the fact that he could not work through these issues unless his mother was ready, too, and that this might or might not happen.

My final session with George was a painful one for me. The aim of my therapy work with George was to help him understand and work through his scapegoated role in the family and its carryover in other situations. I realized that I could not make up to George for the love he had missed and was only partially successful in helping him work through his feelings about not having that love.

UNHOOKING EMMA: A LONGITUDINAL VIEW

An Inconspicuous Young Woman

Emma was a thin, tall, pale twenty-eight-year-old woman with dark hair and dark eyes. She almost seemed to fade into the wall while she stood waiting for me. I came out to greet her and, for a moment, missed her as my eyes went past her; she seemed so inconspicuous.

Emma walked with me to my office and mentioned that the only reason she had decided to come was because she had seen me elsewhere and felt that she could relate to me. I was happy at this show of confidence. Thus began my journey with Emma.

Emma had an older brother, but she was the eldest daughter in a family of six children. She described her father, Gilbert, as an old, overbearing Navy man who ruled the family with an iron hand whenever he was around them.

Emma's mother, Carol, was 22 years younger than her father. Gilbert had met and married Carol in Italy. Emma related this family history without any affect. However, her voice showed some liveliness when she started to talk about Carol. She described her mother as a beautiful woman, as "beautiful as Liz Taylor," adding that she knew how to use her beauty. Her father was away from home for long periods of time with Navy assignments and Carol looked after herself and her children. Gilbert sent home money regularly; however, Carol felt that she was missing out on her social life.

The Chaotic Home Atmosphere

From childhood, Emma remembered that her mother talked negatively about her father, saying that Carol had been fooled into marrying him and that he was really an old man who could not satisfy her in any way. The only reason Carol remained married to him was out of gratitude as she had been able to bring her younger sisters and her aunts into this country.

By the time Emma was six years of age, she had three younger sisters and recollections of a painful childhood. Emma's earliest recollection of her father was that of an angry, bullying man whose presence made everyone very quiet. He would bellow and order Carol around. Everything had to be in its place, and what Emma remembered distinctly was his temper when he could not get through to someone. Emma remembered her father being angry with her for some reason or another and always telling her she was the ugliest child he had ever seen in his life, thus picking on her physical features and scapegoating her. Emma started to feel condemned from a very young age.

The father said that he would like to beat the hell out of her but added sarcastically that she was so ugly he did not know how he could bring himself to do it. Often he ordered Emma to leave the dining table, complaining angrily that he could not bear to see her face. Many times Emma said that she cried herself to sleep, but no one came to console her. Often she had heard her parents quarreling. Her mother would start to cry and then the fighting would taper off. Soon after such incidents, her father would be out of the house for long periods of time, drinking in a bar. Emma remembers her father as being in and out of the family due to his Navy assignments.

As time passed, Emma became aware that her mother had a number of friends, both men and women, and Emma had "to keep an eye on the children to see that nothing went wrong." When the phone rang, or if any of the children questioned her, Emma was told to explain that they had to be on their best behavior because her mother's friends were visiting. Later on, Carol got into the habit of going away from home with friends and leaving her children with her sister's husband, Joseph, who was unemployed. He would come home and take care of Emma and her siblings.

Emma's Outlook

Let me stop here and tell you how I felt about this client. I felt sorry for her. It seemed like Emma had lost out in life; the victimized aspect of herself was very revealing: in fact, the attitude she projected made her seem like she was trying to hide something. Emma's affect was always dull and when she spoke, every word she said seemed to draw the breath out of her. There was something missing in her story when she talked about herself. Perhaps it was my intuition at work, but I felt that she was avoiding something. So I questioned her, saying that I could help her best if she openly discussed with me all the issues in her life that had been significant. Emma mentioned that she did not like her uncle and then put her head down. She talked in monosyllables about problems in her life. As the session came to an end, we set up an appointment to meet the following week. She looked at me and stated that she would write to me. Because the appointment was for the following week, I asked her why

she wished to write. Emma smiled weakly, mumbled
something hurriedly, and then left.

The Letter

A few weeks after I had been seeing Emma, I received
her letter. In this letter she explained that she had seen a
therapist before but had dropped out of therapy because
it was very painful. At the end of the letter, almost as an
afterthought, she wrote in very tiny words that she had
been in an incestuous relationship with her uncle from
age five until her sixteenth birthday. That was one of the
reasons that her father had thrown her out of the house
when she finished high school and her mother did not
support her financially.

In the fifth session, Emma complained of a headache
and mentioned that she felt depressed. For her it was an
awful effort to put on her clothes and come for therapy.
She said that she had a job where she had to work day
and night shifts and this affected her health. There had
been major stressors in her life, with serious adjustments
to a new job and an unresolved family situation that added
to her feelings of depression. Emma made no mention of
the letter she had written, so I brought it up. She started
to cry and asked me, in a scared and helpless manner,
what I thought of the letter. Though she asked about the
letter, her voice betrayed her fear that I might reject her
for her "badness." So carefully I said that I could see how
bad she felt and her desire to avoid a face-to-face discussion
was understandable. I went on to say that I did not believe
that she was responsible for what happened to her as a
child. I reassured her that the purpose of therapy was to
help her handle her life differently and meaningfully, and

that I was there to help her and not to judge her life situations.

Emma started to talk about the incest, at first hesitantly, but then the words poured out of her like a tornado, as if she had to complete the story quickly, as if she were not sure that I would be available to her again. Emma started her story by saying that her mother was never home and that at times when she was at home, she was busy. Her uncle Joseph, who used to baby-sit the children, would take Emma underneath the staircase, which she remembered as always dark, and made her participate in different types of sexual activities. When he was done, he would tell her not to talk about it to anyone because it would create problems in the family. Emma believed him because she knew that her parents always quarreled, and she was afraid that her revelation would break up the home.

Marital Conflicts

Meanwhile, whenever Emma's parents had a problem, Carol would run to Emma, apparently the parentified child, and complain about her husband, Gilbert. As explained in Chapter 2, the blurring of generational lines can be expressed by *parentification*: the reversal of parent-child roles where the child is allowed to gain power over the parent(s) because of his or her ability to satisfy the parent's needs. These needs can be long-term unsatisfied parental wishes and desires actually directed toward the parent's own parents. The child is delegated to refurbish the parent's waning feelings of self-worth, to protect the parent, and to take care of the siblings. The child performs the role as she or he feels loyal to the parent.

This was true of Emma; she was her mother's protector

and confidante. Carol told Emma, with callous frankness, how she was waiting to divorce her husband because he was an evil man. Carol constantly complained that she was very young in comparison to her husband and really needed to be with a younger man. Emma was used to her mother's lamenting about her father and always wondered why her mother put up with all the pain she felt. There was a strong cross-generational coalition between mother and daughter. In this family, the marital problems were poorly resolved and the mother united with Emma in a coalition against her spouse, keeping him peripheral or making him overcontrol (Minuchin & Fishman, 1981). Emma was very empathetic to her mother's problems and really did not seem to care about her father.

Emma—the Victim

To Emma's surprise one day, when her father and mother were fighting, Carol, who was very impulsive, told Gilbert that Emma at age 8 also thought that he was not a good father and had wondered if her parents should even remain married. This was not true. However, Gilbert immediately ran to Emma, who was sitting in the kitchen, and started to beat her. Carol intervened but only after Emma had been beaten blue and black. Emma felt that her father disliked her but now there was proof. She cried as she related the story. Emma felt sorry for her mother who had put up with this man, and did not blame her mother for making up stories or for anything else. Her ability to see her mother as a person without defects was mind-boggling. However, looking at Emma, it was clear that she thought of herself as her mother's savior. Her mother had unwittingly placed Emma in this role, and

Emma had willingly, or perhaps unconsciously, accepted this role. As a parentified child, she took on a number of adult responsibilities. With a helpless gaze, she looked at me, and repeated relentlessly that her mother was a young person compared to her father and she needed to be protected from him. Thus, Emma was the family burden bearer and the family scapegoat.

How did Emma's relationships progress in her family? Whenever she sat in a room and her father walked in, he would order her out of the room, saying that he could not bear to see her ugly face. If she was sitting in the living room with her other siblings, he would yank her out of the room, saying that she was making the room ugly. What she distinctly remembers of her father was the fact that he persistently called her "ugly."

Emma was quiet for a few minutes and then started to cry. I did not interrupt her. She added that she felt ugly because her father did not like her and her uncle used her whenever he visited them or did baby-sitting for them, which was frequently. One of the few times Emma looked me straight in the eyes was when she said she was really ugly. Her "ugliness" was part of a negative body image that Emma had internalized into her personality. She continued to say that she hated what her uncle had done to her, but she had not told her mother because she felt that her mother was too frail. Emma hated her uncle and had tried to avoid him but could not do so because she was alone in the house with him. Her uncle would successfully distract Emma's older brother with errands and send the younger children to play in the yard. Emma felt that she had no control over anything in her own home while her uncle was around, because he was so smart in getting what he wanted.

One day when her uncle came to visit, he sarcastically told Emma that her mother was having an affair with a man in the house. Though Emma knew her mother had a number of male friends, somehow she did not really think that her mother could be unfaithful to her father. Emma did not believe her uncle and ran upstairs, impelled to see for herself that her uncle lied. But to her horror, she surprised her mother who was in bed with a stranger. Running out of the room, Emma started to cry. Carol told Emma later that she disliked Gilbert because he was a very cruel man and that she wanted to marry this man who had been in bed with her. Emma was convinced by her mother that what Carol was doing was good for the family.

Mother's Confidante

From that time on, Emma's role in the family changed. She became more and more her mother's confidante and went with her mother and her boyfriend to the movies and on other outings. After some time, when her mother grew tired of this boyfriend, another man came into her life, and so it continued. Throughout this discussion Emma apologized for her mother and her behavior, saying again and again, almost like a parrot, that her mother desired better and, therefore, there was nothing wrong in her going out with other guys. Emma played her role of the scapegoat remarkably well. She always bent backwards to accommodate her mother's faults but would not tolerate any faults in her own behavior. Emma's support of her mother was amazing. Even when Carol told on Emma to her father, Emma found excuses for her mother's behavior, explaining that Carol was afraid of her father, that he was a tyrant and so forth. On the other hand, she saw her father as a person who embodied all the evil. This was very similar to the accuser-victim aspects of her personality. Father was the cruel accuser and Mother was the downtrodden victim. Throughout the therapy session Emma never once made a negative comment about her mother. In fact she was very protective toward her. My slightest suggestion of anything negative about her mother would bring a torrent of protest, but a few minutes later she would forgive me, too, as I did not know any better.

When Gilbert returned home from a tour of duty, Carol got pregnant again, but Emma heard rumors from the next-door neighbors that the child could not be her father's. Emma believed the rumors to be true, because her last two siblings, a younger sister and the youngest brother, did not resemble the rest of the family. Emma was hoping that her mother would divorce Gilbert because of their incessant marital conflicts, but this did not happen.

One day when her father was home, Emma and her older brother had a big fight. The brother, in a fit of fury, screamed that he would tell their father that Emma accompanied Carol whenever she went out with men. These men were bad and Emma was encouraging her mother to be unfaithful to their father. Emma was aghast with fear. She cried and begged her brother not to tell their father, but he did, rather impulsively, and Emma thoughtfully added to this information, without thinking of the repercussions; then, all hell broke loose on Emma. She was victimized a second time.

At first the father tried to choke his wife. Emma felt that she was also responsible as she had gone out with the mother, so she intervened to help her mother, who was tearing at her husband's clothes. Emma pushed her father away, and he turned around and started to beat her. He told her that he wanted her out of the house permanently, as soon as possible. He added that he never wanted to see her face again. She was a 13-year-old at that time. Emma ran out of the house, and was met by her uncle who happened to be coming home. After consoling her, he took her to his car and repeatedly used her sexually throughout that evening.

Emma hated her uncle and could not tell anyone about it. She felt trapped: everybody seemed to point a finger at her for all the troubles in the family. When her sisters were not well, she was blamed; if her mother was not well, she was also blamed. She grew tired of this life, she said, and giving me the rare twinkle in her eyes, added quickly that she would always be available for Carol. That was the only reason for Emma to return back home—to be her mother's friend and supporter.

End of Incest

By the time Emma reached her sixteenth year, she was very tired of her uncle and his vulgar ways. One day she threatened to tell on him; he angrily replied that no one would believe her, for he knew she was equally responsible for whatever happened between them.

On her sixteenth birthday, her mother gave her a blue dress; Emma liked herself in it and walked to the woods near her house where she sat down on the grass, contemplating life. Emma described herself as a moody person. Her uncle walked up to her and greeted her with, "Hey, big girl, where did you get that dress?" Emma was tired of him. She wanted to go out with boys of her own age, so she told him to shut up and leave her alone. He got angry, ran up to her, and told her that because she had turned 16 did not mean her relationship with him was over because they still had their "little secret." He insisted she also had to do whatever he told her because nobody else would have her. Cruelly he added that she was ugly, just what her father had said repeatedly.

This made Emma very angry, because she felt that her uncle was being mean like her father. She also knew in the back of her mind that her uncle had misused her and not allowed her to have any friends, girls or boys, because he always turned up at the wrong places, like at her school. She felt embarrassed and afraid that everyone would find out about her and her dirty ways. Emma had come to a point of no return with her uncle. She hated him, so she got up and started to scratch at him and scream and cry. She did not think anyone in the house would see or hear them, but someone did. I asked her if she had fought with the uncle in this fashion before. She replied affirm-atively saying that she had gotten into fights with him a few times before this, but never this overt and loud. However, her mother came to her side, while Emma was crying and screaming.

To her mother's hysterical weeping and questioning, Emma blurted out what she always wanted to tell her— that her uncle had been doing sexual things to her from the time she was a child. Her mother was shocked and did not believe Emma, because Joseph was her younger sister's husband. Carol turned against Emma and screamed that she was obnoxious for telling lies. The uncle claimed that Emma had always talked to him like an adult and did not know where she got her ideas. He then started to weep like he was a child. His masking of the issue worked. Amid this turmoil, her father joined them and ordered Emma to go home and wait for him. Nobody believed what she said, and the adults were very supportive of the uncle saying that Emma was used to being tricky.

The Outsider in the Family

At home, her father told her in a deliberate voice to get her things from her room and leave them in the kitchen. She was no longer to sleep in the bedroom with her sisters but on the kitchen floor. When Emma finished school, the father wanted her to leave home and never return, as she caused problems not only for her uncle, but also for her mother and for himself by her deceptive ways. Her mother did not offer any support. By now I was aware of Emma's pattern of supporting her mother. Emma apologized for her mother, repeating that Carol was afraid of Gilbert; Emma hoped that her mother would leave him as he was an old man and her mother was still very young and needed to experience life differently. This is typical of the scapegoat's behavior. They readily find reasons for everyone's problems and can be understanding toward them to points of defection but will not tolerate any weaknesses in themselves. Not once did Emma say that her mother had used her to cover up her problems or that Carol was not really supportive of her.

True to his word, when Emma finished high school, her father put her out of the house. All the money she had was her meager earnings from a fast food restaurant. But her father was firm and told Emma never to return home for any reason. He was true to his word. Even when she called home, he disconnected the line. By this time he was retired and at home, so Emma could not even sneak by to see her mother. However, in the beginning of her exile, she had managed to talk to her mother on the phone a few times. Carol always complained about Gilbert and added that she was waiting for all the children to grow up so that she could leave him. Emma was still waiting for her mother to leave her father after ten years. However, Emma believed more and more that Carol would not leave Gilbert, as she was getting old and did not know how to survive by herself.

Emma's Strengths

Emma, who was always called ugly and sometimes stupid by her father, still wished to prove to him that she was bright and smart; she earned an undergraduate degree and then a graduate degree. The desire to please her rejecting father was intense. She had the satisfaction of talking to her father recently and telling him what she was doing with her life, and as much as this was against his will, he was pleasantly surprised that she got an education. Carol now worked at a fast food restaurant, and Emma saw her sometimes. Emma has never been invited to go home, but she sneaked in to see her mother a few times. Her parents did not help her financially, but Emma managed to pay for her education with part-time jobs and scholarships. Today she considers herself a bright person, though her affect, style of communication, and behaviors reveal a very troubled person.

Problems Worked On in Therapy

One of the problems Emma brought to therapy was her inability to date men. She had never had a date, was very reluctant to communicate with any man, except her boss, and did not know what she wanted to do with herself. She constantly complained that she was depressed and wished to know how to get rid of her depression. These forms of behavior were the result of the emotional, sexual, and physical scapegoating that Emma suffered while growing up and her present uncertainties about life. We worked on her depression, which was the result of her chronic conflicts with her family, her unresolved position, and her role as scapegoat. Intellectually, Emma was bright, but emotionally she was like a lost child. I worked with her, attempting to unhook her from the scapegoated role that she carried with her.

As mentioned previously, Emma presented herself in therapy as a lifeless person with no enthusiasm. She said that her younger brother was treated badly after she left home, and when he left home, the parents picked on the second to last child, who was "very different in her ways." Emma was unaware that she was talking about the interlocking triangles present in the family. After several sessions, my herculean task seemed easier when I explained to Emma—and she vigorously agreed as time passed—that her parents had issues of their own and a lack of understanding and harmony in the marriage and, therefore, used the children to keep themselves together as a couple.

From the time Emma began therapy, I attempted to reach her mother, for it appeared that Emma could not take complete charge of her life without her mother's support and approval. The mother broke the appointment three times and her reasons varied. As there was no possibility of getting Emma's parent or parents involved in therapy, I worked toward helping Emma accept her parents the way they were. Emma seemed resigned to this plan, as she had seen this happen with her earlier therapist.

The next best thing that could happen was helping Emma understand her parents' issues and fears and the lack of togetherness in their marriage. Emma had specialized in understanding human behavior in college and mentioned that she was aware of her parents' problems. I assumed, based on her presentation of self, that she understood her issues intellectually. The difficult part for me was to help her understand and accept her situation emotionally and then move on in life.

The Family Myth

The family myth can be described as the set of role images that are accepted by the whole family together as representing each member; each allotted role gives each person a particular way of behaving and interacting (Pillari, 1986). The roles of some of the children in this particular family were those of scapegoats so that the husband and wife could camouflage their own issues under the mask of the children's problems. There were many family legends present in the family. Family legends as Byng-Hall (1988) describes them are colored and colorful stories that are told time and time again—in contrast to other information about the family's past, which fades away. Although the legends are told ostensibly because they are interesting, frequently the way they are told indicates how the family should behave. With each telling of the story, the current rules of the family are encoded and elaborated.

In Emma's family the legend presented all women from the mother's side of the family as very beautiful and, if beautiful, the woman should use her beauty positively to her advantage. In many ways Carol did this for her marriage and for her affairs, in spite of her marital dissatisfaction. She managed to remain married to the same man and enjoy the positive factor of good financial security. Emma did not fit into her family for she was not considered beautiful. We talked about beauty in Emma's family and looked at family photos. Although her mother was very good-looking and so were two of her sisters, the rest of the family did not inherit good looks. So "good-looking" prescribed behavior patterns—which meant with good looks, a person could get away with anything. In the congenial therapeutic relationship as we discussed the family patterns, it appeared as if Emma was developing more insight into her own patterns and into the scape-goating patterns that took place in her family.

Triangulation

Kerr and Bowen (1988) say that there are several ways by which a third person can be incorporated into the family tension. The uncomfortable insider (the mother in this instance) can pull an outsider (Emma, the daughter) into the marital situation through complaints to the out-sider about the other insider (the husband) and vice versa. When Emma responded sympathetically, taking sides with her mother, a comfortable closeness was established be-tween mother and daughter and the father became the outsider. In this situation, the mother and the daughter blamed the father for problems in the relationship between husband and wife. Through years of training, Emma had learned to gravitate toward the disharmony; she seemed to sense tension in her parents very easily. Often a poorly differentiated person may occupy this type of position with his or her parents. Emma predictably made herself into a problem, for example, cutting classes while in junior high, being very stubborn, and so forth, whenever tension reached a certain level between the parents. This drew both parents to focus on Emma and reduced the tension between them.

However, when Emma was asked to leave home, the tension between husband and wife was so great that a son was involved in the situation by the mother's communication to him of her anxiety. Thus another triangle was created. Conflict erupted between father and son when the one who was triangled got the other to "behave." In this situation the son tried to tell the father how controlling and unsympathetic he had been to the mother. Meanwhile, the mother achieved an outside position. So in this situation, because Emma was no longer available, the tension spilled over into another person. As mentioned earlier, this "process," in which anxiety that cannot be contained within one triangle overflows into one or more other triangles, is referred to as interlocking triangulation (Kerr & Bowen, 1988). In a relatively calm family, tensions can generally be contained in one central triangle. But when the stress becomes too great, the anxiety spreads to other family triangles and to triangles outside the family in work and other social systems.

In Emma's case, triangulation had remained part of the family up to this point. I worked with Emma in order to get her detriangulated. It was a tedious process. Detriangulating depends on recognizing the ways by which one is triangulated by others. For instance, Emma's statement, "My father treated me badly and I don't want my sister to have to do anything with him," is the beginning of triangulation.

The triangulation process can be presented either as

subtle messages in the form of facial expressions, body changes, and tones of voice, but in Emma's family, it was overt as expressed by the father but somewhat covert as expressed by the mother. Kerr and Bowen see detriangulation as a way of thinking rather than as a technique. The "way of thinking" refers to a systems conceptualization of human behavior in the social environment. Without ascribing the cause of a problem to a particular person or want, the emotional process links people and events and keeps them in focus. When a person develops the capacity to see systems or process, and develops an emotional neutral attitude about the relationship process between others, that person will find it easier to detach himself or herself from a triangulated relationship (Kerr & Bowen, 1988).

The Beginning of the Healing Process

Thus, Emma, who had been physically out of the family picture, had to be helped to understand that her own neutrality or detachment from the family could be achieved by being in contact with the triangles that she is most connected to emotionally. She could then act on the basis of neutrality. Despite Emma's negative feelings toward her father, she had to understand for the equally important purposes of detriangulating and differentiating herself that she continue to be in contact with this relationship, without triggering feelings and attitudes that were part of the earlier process. Emma began to call and talk to her father, at first diffidently, and she kept herself neutral in terms of family issues. Later she was able to talk a little more comfortably about her academic achievements, and he appeared to be proud of her in this realm.

In an atmosphere of blamelessness, the healing process began. In order to help Emma, it was important to create a link between the past and the present and to help her see her role in the family of origin as a nonfamily person. Even though Emma had taken on the responsibility for her family's desires and needs, she viewed herself as being distinctly different from the rest of the family. One of the important aspects of healing was to help Emma acknowledge this self-view as nonfamily, followed by her realization of the connections between the act of being scapegoated and the dynamics of the family of origin.

I used role play and enactment to help Emma understand her family situation. Enactment is the perception of the patterns of the family dance by the therapist. In this case, based on Emma's family patterns, I created scenarios, facilitating the enactment of familiar movements by the use of empty chairs that were given the names Mother, Father, Uncle and Brother. I constructed an interpersonal scene in which dysfunctional patterns in the family were played out; this was used to show Emma that she had been pulled into the family situation as the mother's nurturer and supporter and the father's enemy. Emma was helped to understand the problems in the marital relationship between her parents and how she had unwillingly and unwittingly became drawn in.

The incest relationship and its issues were discussed with her earlier therapist and, as Emma developed more trust in me, she started to talk about her uncle. He had abused other young children and, when his behavior was exposed, the family was overcome with shame. Finally, he and his family left the area and moved to a town in the West. This had happened about four years ago; Emma said that she was very relieved he was no longer in town, although, she added quickly, she would deal with him differently at this point in her life. There were many issues in her life which were the result of the incestuous relationship: her inability to make friends with men, her severe physical appearance, her style of dressing like a boy, and her total mistrust of men, in which I am aware her father played a part as well, due to his disapproval of her, even as a child.

In discussing aspects of this case, I should also mention that the relationship I had with Emma started to change as time passed. At first she was really timid and shy but later she developed a great liking for me. It started as gratitude when she thanked me for being her therapist. At a later point she watched me with admiration. As time passed, Emma got more comfortable with me and worried that she was not dating. With my encouragement she made a few half-hearted efforts. She would discuss how she should dress and I would encourage her in this venture, for perhaps this was the first time she saw herself as a woman. Emma learned to use lipstick, wore dresses more often, and made special efforts to meet men. She would come dressed up for therapy and, in a childlike manner, wait for my opinion.

I believe transference had taken place, and at times I wondered if her attraction to me was sexual because she was more comfortable with women than with men. I brought up the question of sexuality, but she was extremely uneasy, so I tucked away this question for another day when she would be ready for it. I decided that Emma would have to make her sexual choices in her personal life. She had a tremendous awareness that her childhood had negatively exploited her, but she realized this was her past and it could not be changed with time. . . . Emma slowly developed an ability to live with it.

Emma also had to deal with the here-and-now, as this

was where she was firmly rooted. One of the issues was to help her deal with her sexuality in a way in which she would be comfortable and to help her adjust herself to her life and move on. Based on the congenial therapeutic relationship, the transference factors, and Emma's progress in therapy, I was confident that most of her problems would be worked through constructively.

THE WALKERS: THERAPEUTIC ALLIANCES AND RESTRUCTURING THE FAMILY

A United Front

The Walker family and I met at least two times. Most of the time the family members were quiet, well behaved, and polite; I was not sure why they were in therapy with the 14-year-old son, Leo—later identified as the problem child—since they presented such a united front. However, after the first two sessions and the father's departure, the family dynamics began to change and, much to my relief, there was a breakthrough: six-foot-tall, stalwart, grave Leo, who was always in control of himself, broke down and cried saying that his mother had beaten him a week ago. When Leo's mother Cindy looked surprised, he added, in between uncontrollable sobs, that she even wanted him to leave home. I valued these moments, because after weeks of quiet, obedient silence and appropriate comments, Leo at last was able to speak for himself when encouraged. This behavior was very different compared to his earlier subdued affect. He was beginning to show confidence and trust in me.

A Brief Family History

In the first two sessions, both parents and their four children came in for therapy. However, after the second session, the father Greg had to leave for overseas duty. As mentioned earlier, after the father's departure, the family dynamics and situation started to change. Leo was the oldest child and the only stepchild in the family. He had been born out of wedlock when his mother, Cindy, was 17. He lived with her by himself until the age of six. According to Cindy, Leo's father, Kevin, was an alcoholic and an irresponsible man. He had promised to marry Cindy when she became pregnant and he constantly swore that he loved her. However, a week before their scheduled marriage, he came to visit Cindy with another girlfriend, who obstrusively claimed that Kevin was to marry her. Cindy was devastated, but she had too much pride to show it. She returned to her parents' home and lived there until she had Leo and was able to provide for herself as a single parent.

When Leo was six years of age, Cindy met her present husband, Greg. Three children were born of this marriage. Greg attempted to adopt Leo, but Leo's natural father, who had seen Leo only three times in his life, refused to give Cindy legal permission and later disappeared. Leo was, therefore, in limbo and Greg, his stepfather, could not help him unless they went through a tedious legal process. Greg, who was a military officer, spent about six months of the year on overseas duty.

The Chosen Victim

Thus, we come back to the session when Leo broke down about the incident that happened when his stepfather was away. Leo was gentle and affable, but his present behavior revealed citadels of wrath and pain. It seemed to me that his mother tried to pacify him because she was mostly embarrassed that he was complaining about her. But pacification did not ensue, and Leo continued to cry, repeating that he had always been treated differently. Cindy, who was generally quite talkative, was painfully quiet in the presence of her son's conscious anger. Leo explained that he did more chores in the home than the other children, and if he was a few minutes late in doing his chores, his mother would jump at him. He was aware of other blasphemies that were present in the family. As he gained more control of the session, he added with a supercilious smile that I should ask his mother about Greg, and then he refused to speak any further.

Cindy took over and mentioned that Leo was right that his stepfather, Greg, had a violent temper and had broken a door and the TV set in their family room when he was home the last time. After that comment, Cindy continued in a matter-of-fact manner, emphasizing that she was strict with Leo because she did not want him to become like her husband Greg, who had a drinking problem and a violent temper. Leo started to cry and complained that Cindy loved her other children more than she loved him and he was always treated differently. Unlike earlier examples in which the scapegoated persons accepted their roles, in Leo's case it was different. He had been pampered when he lived alone with his mother and he wanted his former position back.

Cindy had always presented herself as an affable, caring person, and she was distraught with her son's behavior. Talking about an earlier incident, she added that when she asked Leo to pack and leave the house, she wanted him to go and live with his grandmother who lived in another state. I explained that telling a child in a fit of temper to live with someone else only shows the child that he was being rejected, as if he were not good enough to live at home. This comment pushed the mother to communicate more information. She argued limply that she did this when he threatened to run away from home.

Sibling Relationships

With painful tears in his eyes, Leo complained that his mother often beat him and always seemed to find fault with him. Greg, his stepfather, was the same. When there were quarrels between Leo and his younger brother, Fred, Leo would be blamed and invariably punished, but his brother would go unpunished. By this time, Cindy had become quieter, but she intervened saying that since Leo was older he was supposed to set a good example. Leo mentioned that his younger brother was eight years old, but there were no rules in the family for him. He angrily added that Fred could do anything he wanted and get away with it. Moreover, Leo cried that his younger brother bossed him around, but his parents did nothing about this.

I believe, as Kahn and Lewis (1988) relate, that from a very young age siblings begin to rely on each other for contact and companionship. Siblings become each other's agents for intense emotional experience. In their mutual self-object relationships, needs for love, hate, yearning, hope, envy, anger, merging, mirroring, idealization, and identification are partially, but incompletely, gratified. Oftentimes, parents are oblivious to any or all emotional transactions between the children, content as long as the children can "play" together and not make noise; they move to action only if "fighting" reaches intense proportions (Kahn & Lewis, 1988). Whenever this fighting started between Leo and Fred, their mother would rush to Fred's rescue. The relationship between Leo and Fred was discontinuous, disruptive, and disharmonious.

To my question of whether Leo felt less loved by his parents, he responded by aggressively nodding his head. Perhaps due to his earlier role in the single-parent family with his mother until the age of six, he had experienced a more nurturing environment, and therefore at the current point in time, he was protesting against his newly assigned role of scapegoat. Cindy continued to protest that she loved all of the children in a similar fashion, which I believe is a myth that most parents would like their children to accept. I suggested that the rest of the children, that is, Fred and his younger twin brother and sister, Andy and Alicia, be allowed to participate actively in therapy, as Cindy was inclined (and requested me) to send the younger children to the play room and to focus on Leo as the problem. It was clear that Leo felt like the odd one out and was, of course, the scapegoat, for it appeared that he was the one person who was singled out as the cause of family problems and was thus the recipient of family anger (Pillari, 1986). This also seemed to stem from the fact that Leo was thwarted and exposed as the child of a different father. Scapegoating, as has been noted, seems to happen when a difference is noted.

Siblings in Therapy

However, in the following session, it became clear that the younger brother, Fred, saw himself as having more power than his older brother, Leo. Fred made comments that implied he knew everything that Leo knew and could do. It appeared that Leo, as the child of a single parent and later with his stepfather at sea, had developed an overburdened parental role with more chores to perform. This was greatly resented by his younger brother who felt the need to constantly challenge Leo. To Leo's amazement and pain, he found that he was being slowly displaced by his brother, Fred, for their mother gave Fred more importance in her own elusive ways. Though there were volcanic outbursts from Fred against Leo, the mother remained obstinately silent. Though Fred was short, about four feet three inches tall, and Leo at six feet towered over him, Fred was indescribably offensive to Leo. Leo, who was looking for support from his mother, did not receive it, so he withdrew with mellow sadness.

Meanwhile in the family session, Fred also appeared to be very distracted. He commented that he liked to draw. I find that art therapy tasks are adaptable to the many aspects of family therapy—for instance, unlayering the participant's earlier experiences, exploring the family of origin, examining past and current histories, surfacing preconscious material, reducing defenses, gaining insight and emotional configurations, pointing out dysfunctional behaviors, differentiating family members, uncovering conflict, improving parenting and problem-solving skills, and coping with grief and mourning (Landgarten, 1987). Art therapy may also designate directives that manipulate a trial realignment of subsystems and change boundaries.

So I asked Fred to draw a picture of himself and his older brother. It was interesting that Fred presented himself as a taller person and his older brother as a shorter person. As I wished to bring about change actively, I used a structural intervention that would purposefully interrupt the family's usual transactional behavior and require family members to rearrange their roles (Minuchin, 1974).

I then orchestrated a scene. I asked Fred to stand on a chair next to his brother, which he did. Even while standing on the chair, Fred was still shorter than Leo. When I pointed this out to Leo and Fred, Leo smiled in an embarrassed manner. Later I made them stand next to each other on the ground and, at this time, Fred exclaimed that Leo was taller. I talked to both of them briefly about their power struggles. At this point the mother intervened to say that Leo had a problem as he always compared himself to Fred and worried about not having enough privileges.

On this day Leo appeared to be in a talkative mood, and he complained about the mistreatment and lopsided justice that existed in the family. When no family member took him on, he hesitantly lapsed into silence. I wondered if any conscious effort could be made to change the rules in the family because Leo literally had no freedom to do anything in the family. Cindy, in tears, complained that she had other problems that weighed her down and perhaps she was being overly strict with Leo. For me, this was the second breakthrough. The mother had acknowledged her humanness and her ability to make mistakes. I gave them an assignment requiring Cindy and Leo to hug each other at least once a day, until we met the next time, for Leo had complained that he was not loved by his mother and she did not hug him at all. She agreed with amused tolerance and Leo maintained a stony silence.

Cindy's Childhood

In the next session, Cindy mentioned that they had not carried through with the assignment. She was thoughtful and filled with remorse. She talked insightfully about the manner in which she had treated Leo, saying that it was very similar to the manner in which she was treated at home while growing up. Thus, Cindy began to talk about her own childhood. Her family rarely hugged, and Cindy had a large number of responsibilities from a very young age. She took care of her younger siblings, a brother and two sisters. Cindy revealed that her father, who had a drinking problem, used to make sexual comments to her even when she was as young as six years old and her mother, Lila, would be upset with Cindy and not with the father, claiming that Cindy was attempting to get his attention.

As Cindy grew older, if she dressed well or was humorous in front of her father, her mother would suspect that Cindy was attempting to be seductive. Cindy did not remember ever being hugged by her mother and her father was not allowed to touch his daughters. There was a family secret that Cindy had still not penetrated. Her older sister, whom she remembers slightly, ran away from home when she was just 11 years old. Cindy's mother would never explain what happened, except to say that the girl had done the right thing. Cindy had often wondered if this daughter had been sexually abused by her father.

Cindy remembered an incident that happened when she was 12, immediately after she reached puberty. While taking a bath, she felt like someone was watching her. Her uneasiness was sadly rewarded when she noticed that the outside bathroom window was open, and her father, an untidy and grotesque spectacle, was watching her. Cindy quickly wrapped a towel around herself and screamed at him, angrily warning him that he should never open the window again. She was astounded by the pain of being robbed of her childhood, for she remembers that when she complained to her mother, Lila looked at her accusingly as if she had done something wrong. Thus, it became clear that Cindy's mother was overly protective of her husband and her marriage, and Cindy believes that at a very young age she received a number of subtle messages to protect and take care of her brother and sisters.

So Cindy played the role of the burden-bearer and took physical care of her younger siblings. In spite of being overloaded with responsibilities, she got into trouble if she did not do some basic task like making sure they ate their food. At the same time, she was overwhelmed with work and filled with smoldering guilt, for nothing she did was ever considered to be good enough. At times these feelings caused Cindy's angry outbursts, which got her into deeper trouble with her mother. This gave the mother an opportunity to beguile Cindy and exploit her. Thus, while growing up, Cindy herself had been scapegoated. However, Cindy claimed that she loved her mother, simply because she was her mother.

As seen in earlier examples, the scapegoated victim, Cindy, desired to give her mother all the support she would give. However, the mother leaves Cindy feeling empty and sets the stage for the child to experience a loss of positive self-identity. The negative self-image of Cindy is consistent with her mother's definition of Cindy and Cindy, in turn, accepts this negative self-image.

Eventually, when Cindy fell in love and escaped from home, her parents got a divorce. Her mother remarried a man who was very similar to Cindy's natural father in that he made sexual comments to his grown-up stepchildren and grandchildren. As usual, Cindy's mother overlooked his behavior and considered his comments the result of her children's and grandchildren's behavior.

The Family Scapegoat and the Family Savior

Cindy, aware of her role as the family scapegoat and savior, continued her story. Her first boyfriend, Leo's father, walked out on her for another woman. Then along came Greg, whom she married when Leo was six years of age. She was happy for two years. During this time, she gave birth to Fred and became pregnant with her twins, Alicia and Andy. To her utter despair, she found out that Greg was playing around. However, Cindy remembered her mother's ways of dealing with an unfaithful, erratic husband and followed suit. She was stoic about Greg's behavior and waited with mellow expectations that he would change his ways. Cindy continued to find excuses for Greg's behavior under extenuating circumstances. But when Greg's girlfriend, Anita, became pregnant, Greg and Cindy separated at Cindy's insistence. The separation lasted for five years.

It was very difficult for Cindy to make ends meet, but she found a job and took care of her children. She commented that Leo was a big help in those days and she made a number of household decisions with his help. Cindy added at that time she had no misgivings about Leo or his behavior. Meanwhile, Greg continued to be in touch with her but was swamped by loose sex, drugs, and alcohol, similar to Cindy's father and her stepfather who were both heavy drinkers. Greg's girlfriend, Anita, was also on drugs. Eventually when Greg's lover's son was four years of age, Cindy agreed to take care of this child, Dan, and Greg reconciled with her.

Cindy played the martyr and took care of this child for a year. Painfully she remembered that she was robbed of pertinent thinking as she spent more time helping Dan adjust to his new family and neglected her own children. Dan was born to a drug-addicted mother and was an extremely uncontrollable child with incomprehensible destructive anger. In retrospect, Cindy believed she behaved this way to please her husband who suffered from an invincible, appalling temper. However, after a year and a half had passed and Cindy had lost her job because Dan demanded so much time, she decided that he should go back to his mother. Her husband reluctantly agreed. He convinced her that he had had the affair because she was not a good wife, and angrily Cindy added that she accepted this opinion and worked doubly hard to please him. The relationship between Greg and his wife was patched, but it was an ugly patch. In retrospect, Cindy was angry that she had taken care of Dan because he had known his father for four years while her five-year-old twins and Fred were still strangers to Greg. (She omitted Leo.) She mentioned that having Dan in her home placed heavy demands on the rest of the children, who all had to cater to Dan's needs as demanded by Greg, for Dan would otherwise fly into a violent tantrum.

Family Problems

Cindy and Greg went into therapy as a family as Leo was needing more and more attention. He was acting out, disobeying, getting mad at his brothers, and so forth. Greg was overly strict and demanding with Leo. However, Cindy commented that after her husband went on overseas duty, the family situation eased once again. Though she claimed that economically the situation was better, Greg's violent temper took a heavy toll on the family. With her head bent, the mother added that Leo was the target. What she failed to note was that he was also her target, but Cindy herself was a victim, too. Now it appeared to her that Leo's treatment by Greg was a repetition of her own role while she was growing up, caught between her parents. At this point in therapy, Greg had been overseas for three months.

There was another stormy session with Cindy and Leo when Leo started to sob, saying he always felt that his mother did not love him. Desperately, Cindy said she *did* love Leo but did not know how to express it. With tears in her eyes, she said that she wanted to talk to me separately. I agreed. Leo expressed surprise and shock that his mother was vulnerable. He walked out of the room, rather willingly and quietly, and went into the recreation room.

Cindy shared her burdens with me and surprisingly Leo was not one of them: she said that Greg had been at sea for three months and she surreptitiously dropped the hint to me that she did not miss or love him. In fact, the most she felt was relief. When asked how she felt about him when they were newly married, Cindy replied without hesitation that it was always a relief when Greg left. Pensively she added that she never loved him, even before she married him. She had a tremendous fear of him and was afraid to tell him that she did not love him. Later she thoughtfully added that, in all justice, she would have to say she had secretly hoped she could change him. However, this never happened. Now Cindy's attitude toward him was so filled with pent-up anger that she could seriously consider leaving him, particularly after the months of therapy that had enabled her to be more self-assertive than she ever was in her earlier years.

Cindy was growing increasingly tired of being the caretaker of everyone and everything while being the scapegoat if anything went wrong. Greg, like Cindy's mother, could make her feel guilty for everything. She sighed, she was tired. Today she felt she would like to do things for herself, for she was developing a self-awareness of her role in her parents' family and now, in her own family.

Cindy recalled an incident in which she had attempted to tell Greg that she wanted a separation from him (hopefully a permanent one); Greg threatened to commit suicide. Cindy felt that she was hopelessly scapegoated in this situation, for he accused her of anything he could think of. Cindy, as usual, felt overwhelmed with guilt and needed to pacify and take care of Greg and his feelings and not deal with her own feelings. However, at this point in therapy she was aware that Greg used this threat as a form of control against her, but she was afraid to bring up the subject again. Cindy resentfully added that the more she thought of Greg, the more angry and dissatisfied she became. To my question of how she would respond to his statement that he loved her, she sadly said that she could not respond to him at all because she knew that she did not love him. So I gave her an assignment to write down her feelings about Greg and, after a week, to read this over to see if it was still relevant.

Cindy diligently wrote about her husband and faced the inescapable fact that she did not really love him. She related an incident when she called Greg overseas to settle some money matters and found that he was visiting another town at 2:00 A.M. in the morning. This threw her into a frenzy as she did not really trust him. When Greg gave Cindy the reasons for being out of town, all she could think of was that he was having an affair. During this confrontation she blurted out to me that there was no trust in the marriage.

Later, when Greg questioned Cindy about whether she missed him, she said that in all honesty she could not reply positively because she did not really miss him. She began to toy with the idea of leaving him permanently. She does not wish to play the role of the caretaker and the martyr or the scapegoat anymore. Now she talked about finding herself a job so that she could be economically independent, and I was aware that this goal tied in deeply with her desire to leave Greg permanently: whether she would really do this or work through the issues of her marriage remains to be seen.

Change

The relationship with Leo changed and improved too. With her progress in therapy, as she became more insightful, Cindy began to share and present herself as a person who could make mistakes and was not perfect. Her weak points that she used against Leo were brought out in therapy. Cindy recognized that Leo had been scapegoated by both herself and her husband. In the accepting atmosphere of the therapy session, with astounding tranquility and perception, she spoke of setting standards for Leo that he could never reach; she felt that her expectations of him, like her mother's expectations of her, had been unrealistic. She was more willing to compromise her lofty standards as she better understood herself and her attitude toward her son. Leo's role as being responsible for all the children was diminished and, in return, a more relaxed home atmosphere developed. Cindy specified that she was very conscious of these changes in her approach and was going slow with it, while keeping Leo informed.

For the first time in her life, she felt comfortable treating and talking to Leo as a fourteen-year-old adolescent rather than as an overly responsible adult. In a peripheral manner, Cindy briefly informed him about Greg and her attempts to work on their marriage issues, which sometimes oozed out as angry behavior toward the children. Cindy also told Leo that she loved him and that he could hug her and she would attempt to do the same. She laughingly told me that when he hugged her, she stiffened up as she had not been hugged while growing up. However, Leo did not become upset and did not think that his mother did not love him. He has learned that his mother's upbringing had no display of overt affection, so he better understood his mother's distancing, aloof behavior. So when he hugged her and she stiffened, he merely smiled, accepting it as her issue and not as a rejection of him. Cindy quickly added that she did not tell Leo anything about her negative feelings toward her marital relationship, though she assumes all the children are in some way aware of them.

Throughout the months of therapy, I gave different assignments to Cindy and Leo. One assignment was for the mother to give the son permission to play with his friends in the evening, which was not permitted earlier. The other three children had to participate in simple household chores. If the children fought with each other, all of them would be punished accordingly, rather than singling out Leo for the punishment. This eventually helped to unhook Leo as the disobedient child. Leo liked these assignments immensely; he felt that for the first time in his life he was being treated fairly.

There have been some subtle structural changes with role differentiation and realignments between different family members. Leo and his mother continue to work on their relationship and their family issues together and separately. It is safe to say that there has been a lot of insight, growth, and interdependence in this family.

As seen in these three different cases, the ability of the clients to change and grow varied. In all cases the therapist attempted and enabled the client's personality to develop. These clients learned that action, desire, and pain are part of life and should not be branded negatively. It was found that such acceptance and objectivity were themselves psychologically nourishing. The capacity to endure and a willingness to risk change and to play freely with possibilities without shame were fostered in the healing process.

Finally it can be said that dealing with human pain has its seasons: seasons of sadness, anger, hostility, fear, and hope. Fortunately, these seasons do not follow one another in a lockstep fashion. One day, a client might show that all the dark clouds have lifted, but the next day something happens and the dark clouds are back. At one moment in therapy, scapegoated persons are happy for small, positive steps toward their growth, but at another, tears emerge, easily and rapidly. But most people do survive pain. Everyone does not recover at the same speed. In fact, recovery and change take place slowly.

But if we are patient, we begin to see the signs of healing and the prospect of a better life begins to unfold. How does this happen? As in the gathering dusk of a dusty evening, we may misunderstand the things we perceive in front of us at a distance, but on moving closer to the objects with an enquiring mind, we realize their true worth and either value them or drop them as useless. In a similar manner, in therapy, the scapegoated person begins to distinguish between what is real and acceptable and what is false and needs to be put away.

In conclusion, this is what I tell scapegoated people who are in the midst of healing to think about:

> Go deep inside yourself
> Find that treasure that
> is known by your name.

> Look at this treasure
> Look at the resources
> that are universal.
> You have them all.

> You can see
> think
> hear
> feel
> taste
> smell
> choose
> move
> sort

> To *sort*—the ability to
> let go of that which once fit
> but no longer does, and
> see clearly what
> fits now.

Now say to yourself,
"I am able,
I can do this.
I have energy through my
groundedness, my relationship to the heavens,
and my interconnectedness with others.
I am able" (Satir, 1985, p. 21).

Bibliography

Ackerman, N. W. (1966). *Treating the troubled family.* New York: Basic Books.

American Heritage Dictionary (2nd College edition) (1982). Boston: Houghton, Mifflin Co.

Balint, M. (1968). *The basic fault.* New York: Brunner/Mazel.

Bertalanffy, Ludwig Von (1934). *Modern theories of development: An introduction to theoretical biology.* London: Oxford University Press.

Bertalanffy, Ludwig Von (1968). *General systems theory.* New York: Braziller.

Boszormenyi-Nagy, I., & Krasner, B. R. (1986). *Between give and take: A clinical guide to contextural therapy.* New York: Brunner/Mazel.

Boszormenyi-Nagy, I., & Spark, G. M. (1973) *Invisible loyalties: Reciprocity in intergenerational family therapy.* New York: Harper & Row. (Reprinted by Brunner/Mazel, New York, 1984).

Bowen, M. (1976) Theory in the practice of psychotherapy. In G. J. Guerin, Jr. (Ed.), *Family therapy: Theory and practice.* New York: Gardner Press.

Bowen, M. (1972). Toward the differentiation of self in one's own family. In J. L. Framo (Ed.), *Family interaction: A dialogue between family researchers and family therapists.* New York: Springer.

Bowen, M. (1978, 1983, 1985). *Family therapy in clinical practice.* New York: Jason Aronson.

Byng-Hall, J. (1988). Scripts and legends in families and family therapy. *Family Process, 27* (2), 167–180.

Doherty, W. J., & Baird, M. A. (1983). *Family therapy and family medicine.* New York: Guilford Press.

Edward, J., Ruskin, N., & Turrini, P. (1981). *Separation-Individuation.* New York: Gardner Press.

Erikson, E. (1968). *Identity, youth and crisis.* New York: Norton.

Firestone, R. W. (1985). *Fantasy bond.* New York: Human Sciences Press, Inc.

Fossum, M. A., & Mason, M. J. (1986). *Facing shame.* New York: Norton.

Frazer, J. G. (1920). *Scapegoat.* New York: Macmillan.

Frazer, J. G. (1922). *The golden bough.* New York: Macmillan.

Freeman, L., & Strean, H. S. (1986). *Guilt.* New York: John Wiley.

Goodwin, D. W. (1985) *Anxiety.* New York: Human Sciences Press, Inc.

Grotstein, J. S. (1985). *Splitting and projective identification.* New York: Jason Aronson.

Henry, J. (1965, 1971). *Pathways to madness.* New York: Random House.

Jung, C. G. (1953–1979). Psychology and alchemy. *Collected works* (20 Vols. Trans.). R. F. C. Hull, H. Read, M. Fordham, G. Adler, & W. McGuire (Eds.). Princeton: Princeton University Press.

Kahn, M. D., & Lewis, K. G. (Eds.) (1988). *Siblings in therapy*: New York: Norton.

Karpel. M. A., & Strauss, E. S. (1983). *Family evaluation.* New York: Gardner Press.

Kerr, M. E., & Bowen, M. (1988). *Family evaluation.* New York: Norton.

Klein, M. (1946). Notes on some schizoid mechanisms. *International Journal of Psychoanalysis, 27,* 99–110.

Laing, R. D. (1965). *The divided self.* New York: Penguin Books.

Landgarten, H. B. (1987). *Family Art Therapy.* New York: Brunner/Mazel.

Large, T. (1989). Some aspects of loneliness in families. *Family Process, 28,* 25–35.

Lederer, W. J., & Jackson, D. D. (1968). *The mirages of marriage.* New York: Norton.

Lidz, T., Cornelison, A., Fleck, S., & Terry, D. (1957). The intrafamilial environment of schizophrenic patients. Marital schism and marital skew. *American Journal of Psychiatry, 114,* 241–248.

Mahler, M., Pine, F., & Bergman, A. (1975). *The psychological birth of the human infant.* New York: Basic Books.

Malan, D. H. (1979). *Individual psychotherapy and the science of psychodynamics.* Boston: Butterworths.

Masterson, J. F. (1985).*The real self.* New York: Brunner/Mazel.

Meissner, W. W. (1980). A note on projective identification. *Journal of American Psychoanalytic Association, 28,* 43–68.

Meltzer, D. (1967). *The psycho-analytic process.* London: Heinemann.

Minuchin, S., & Fishman, H. C. (1981). *Family therapy techniques.* Cambridge, MA: Harvard University Press.

Minuchin, S. (1974). *Families and family therapy.* Cambridge, MA: Harvard University Press.

Minuchin, S., Montalvo, B. G., Rosman, B. L., Schumer, F. (1967). *Families of the slums.* New York: Basic Books.

Ogden, T. A. (1978). A developmental view of identification resulting from maternal impingements. *International Journal of Psychoanalytic Psychotherapy, 7,* 486–508.

Ogden, T. A. (1979). On projective identification. *International Journal of Psychoanalysis, 60,* 357–373.

Okun, B. F., & Rappaport, L. J. (1980). *Working with families.* Belmont: Wadsworth.

Ornston, D. (1978). Projective identification and internal impingement. *International Journal of Psychoanalytic Psychotherapy, 7,* 508–533.

Perera, S. B. (1986). *The scapegoat complex.* Toronto: Inner City Books.

Pillari, V. (1986). *Pathways to family myths.* New York: Brunner/Mazel.

Porton, G. G. (1988). *The World Book Encyclopedia,* Vol. 17. Chicago: The World Books, Inc.

Richter, H. E. (1960). Die narzisztischen Projektionen der Eltern auf das Kind. *Jahrbuch Psychoanalyse, 1,* 62–81.

Richter, H. E. (1963). *Eltern, Kind und Neurose.* Stuttgart: Klett.

Satir, V. (1985). *Meditations and inspirations.* Berkeley: Celestial Arts.

Satir, V. (1972). *Peoplemaking.* Palo Alto: Science & Behavior Books.

Sieburg, E. (1985). *Family communication.* New York: Gardner Press.

Simon, F. B., Stierlin, H., & Wynne, L. C. (1985). *The language of family therapy: A systemic vocabulary and sourcebook.* New York: Family Process Press.

Skynner, R., & Cleese, J. (1983). *Families.* London: Metheun.

Spitz, R. A. (1946). Hospitalism: A follow-up report. *Psychoanalytic Study of the Child, 2,* 113–117.

Stierlin, H. (1959). The adaptation to the "stronger" person's reality. *Psychiatry, 22,* 143–152.

Stierlin, H. (1973). Interpersonal aspects of internalizations. *International Journal of Psychoanalysis. 54.*

Stierlin, H. (1981). *Separating parents and adolescents: A perspective on running away, schizophrenia, and waywardness.* (2nd enlarged edition). New York: Jason Aronson.

Vogel, E. F., & Bell, N. W. (1981). The emotionally disturbed child as the family scapegoat. In R. J. Green & J. L. Framo (Eds.), *Family therapy: major contributions.* New York: International Universities Press.

Watzlawick, P., Beavin, J. H. & Jackson, D. D. (1967). *Pragmatics of human communication.* New York: Norton.

Webster Encyclopedic Unabridged Dictionary of the English Language. (1989). New York: Portland House, Dilithium Press.

Whitmont, E. C. (1986). *Return of the goddess.* New York: The CrossRoad Publishing Co.

Winnicott, D. W. (1986). *Home is where we start from.* Compiled & edited by C. Winnicott, R. Shepard, & M. Davis. New York: Norton.

Winnicott, D. (1948). Pediatrics and Psychiatry, In *Collected papers*, pp. 157–173. New York: Basic Books, 1958.

Wolheim, R. (1969). The mind and the mind's image of itself. *International Journal of Psychoanalysis, 50*, 209–220.

Wynne, L. C., Ryckoff, I. M., Day, J., & Hirsch, S. I. (1958). Pseudomutuality in the family relations of schizophrenics. *Psychiatry, 21*, 205–220.

Index